The Griffle
and Mr. Gotobed

written by SHEILA McCULLAGH
illustrated by MARK CHADWICK

Ladybird Books

One day, Rosa and Pedro,
and Davy and Sarah were all
playing together in Puddle Lane.
Sarah had a gold-colored ball.
She tossed the ball up high.

USING THIS BOOK

One of the best ways of helping children learn to read is to read stories to them and with them. This way they learn what **reading** *is, and they will* gradually come to recognize many words and begin to read for themselves.

First, read the story on the left-hand pages aloud to the child.

Reread the story as often as the child enjoys hearing it. Talk about the pictures as you go.

Later the child will be able to read the words under the pictures on the right-hand pages.

The pages at the back of the book will give you some ideas for helping your child read.

LADYBIRD BOOKS, INC.
Lewiston, Maine 04240 U.S.A.
© Text and layout SHEILA McCULLAGH MCMLXXXV
© In publication LADYBIRD BOOKS LTD MCMLXXXV
Loughborough, Leicestershire, England

Printed in England

Rosa, Davy,
Pedro, and Sarah

The ball went up, into the air.
Mr. Gotobed's bedroom window
was wide open.
The ball went in the open window.

The ball went in
the open window.

"It's gone!" cried Sarah.

"It went in the open window!"

"We have to get it back," said Davy.

"We'll ask Mr. Gotobed," said Pedro.
"Mr. Gotobed won't mind."
Pedro knocked on Mr. Gotobed's door.
Nothing happened.
He knocked again, as hard as he could.

Pedro knocked
on Mr. Gotobed's door.

But Mr. Gotobed didn't hear
the knocking.
He was fast asleep in bed.

Mr. Gotobed was
fast asleep in bed.

"What should we do now?" asked Sarah.
"Grandmother gave me the golden ball.
She'll be very upset,
if we've lost it."

"We haven't lost it," said Rosa.
"We will just have to wait
till Mr. Gotobed wakes up."

"But Grandmother is coming
to see us this afternoon,"
said Sarah.
She knocked on Mr. Gotobed's door.
She knocked as hard as she could.
But Mr. Gotobed didn't wake up.

Sarah knocked
on Mr. Gotobed's door.

Davy saw two green ears
sticking up over the wall
at the end of the lane.
"There's the Griffle!" cried Davy.
"The Griffle will help us!"

"Who is the Griffle?" asked Rosa.

"The Griffle's a friend of mine,"
said Davy.
"He's a vanishing monster.
Look! You can see his ears."

Davy saw
two green ears.

Two green eyes looked over the wall.
"Please come and help us, Griffle,"
said Davy. "We were playing
with Sarah's ball, and the ball
went in Mr. Gotobed's window.
Mr. Gotobed is fast asleep,
and we can't get the ball back."

Two green eyes
looked over the wall.

The ears and the eyes disappeared.
The garden gate
opened and closed,
but they didn't see anyone
come through it.
And then, suddenly,
there was the Griffle!
He was standing in the lane.

the Griffle

"What do you want me to do?"
he asked in a whiffly-griffly voice.

"Could you please get the ball
back for us?" asked Davy.

"I'll try," said the Griffle.
And he disappeared.

"He's gone!" said Rosa.

"No, he hasn't," said Davy.
"He's only vanished.
Watch for his ears."

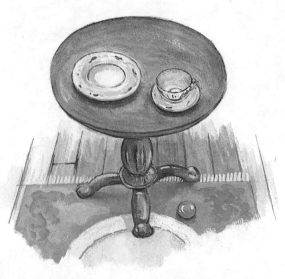

"He has gone!"
said Rosa.

The children looked
at Mr. Gotobed's house.
Sarah saw two green ears
outside Mr. Gotobed's door.
"There he is!" she cried.
The door opened, and
the two green ears disappeared
inside the house.

Sarah saw
two green ears.

Mr. Gotobed was fast asleep in bed.
The door of his bedroom opened,
and the Griffle came in.

Mr. Gotobed was
fast asleep in bed.

The golden ball was lying
right next to Mr. Gotobed's bed.
The Griffle saw the ball.
He went over to it,
and picked it up.

The Griffle
saw the ball.

But as he bent down
to pick up the ball,
his tail bumped into
the little table.
The table fell over.
A cup, a saucer, and a plate
were on the table.
They fell to the floor with a clatter
and a crash.

The table fell over.

Mr. Gotobed woke up.

He saw the Griffle.

Mr. Gotobed woke up.

Mr. Gotobed let out a yell.
"Aah! It must be a dragon!"
cried Mr. Gotobed.
"It must be a dragon!
But where is it now?"
The Griffle had vanished.
The Griffle was gone!

The Griffle was gone!

Mr. Gotobed got out of bed.

He went to the window.

(He didn't see a beautiful golden ball
moving through the air toward
his bedroom door.)

Mr. Gotobed
went to the window.

Mr. Gotobed looked
out the window.
He saw Sarah and Rosa,
and Pedro and Davy,
down in the lane below.
"Have you seen a dragon?"
cried Mr. Gotobed.
"No," said Davy.
"There aren't any **dragons**
in the lane," said Rosa.

Mr. Gotobed looked
out the window.

"I must have been dreaming,"
said Mr. Gotobed.
And he went back to bed.

Mr. Gotobed
went back to bed.

The children saw the door
of Mr. Gotobed's house open.
Two green ears and a golden ball
came out.
The golden ball fell to the ground,
and the two green ears vanished.
"Where are you, Griffle?"
cried Davy.

"It was terrible,"
said a whiffly-griffly voice,
from the other side of the wall.
"Someone shouted at me.
I don't like being shouted at.
I'm going home to get over it."

"I'm so sorry, Griffle," cried Sarah,
as she picked up the ball.
"Thank you **very** much for your help."
There was no answer.
The Griffle was gone.

The Griffle was gone.

Notes for the parent/teacher

When you have read the story, go back to the beginning. Look at each picture and talk about it. Point to the caption below, and read it aloud yourself. Run your finger under the words as you read, so that the child learns that reading goes from left to right. (You don't have to say this in so many words.

Children learn many useful things about reading just by reading with you, and it is often better to let them learn by experience rather than by explanation.)

The next time you go through the book, encourage the child to read the words and sentences under the illustrations. Don't

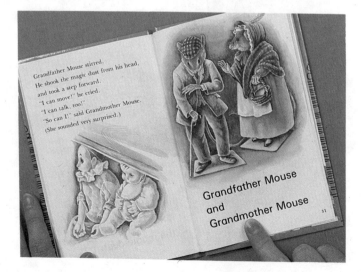

Grandfather Mouse stirred.
He shook the magic dust from his head,
and took a step forward.
"I can move!" he cried.
"I can talk, too!"
"So can I!" said Grandmother Mouse.
(She sounded very surprised.)

Grandfather Mouse
and
Grandmother Mouse

rush in with a word before she* has time to think, but don't leave her struggling for too long. Always encourage her to feel that she is reading successfully, praising her when she does well, and avoiding criticism.

title page, using ordinary, not capital letters. Let her watch you print it: this is another useful experience.

Children enjoy hearing the same story many times. Read this one as often as the child likes hearing it. The more opportunities she has to look at the illustrations and **read** the captions with you, the more she will come to recognize the words. Don't worry if she **remembers** rather than **reads** the captions. This is a normal stage in learning.

Now turn back to the beginning, and print the child's name in the space on the

If you have a number of books, let the child choose which story she would like to hear again.

---

* In order to avoid the continual "he or she," "him or her," the child is referred to in this book as "she." However, the stories are equally appropriate for boys and girls.

There are several books in this Stage about the same characters. All the books in each Stage are separate stories and are written at the same reading level.

You will find other stories about the Griffle and the people in Puddle Lane in these books:

Stage 1

4 Mrs. Pitter-Patter and the Magician

5 The Vanishing Monster

8 Two Green Ears

9 The Tale of a Tail

Mrs. Pitter-Patter

MITZI
and the Elephants

MITZI and the Elephants

by Barbara Williams

**illustrated by
Emily Arnold McCully**

E. P. Dutton   New York

Library of Congress Cataloging in Publication Data

Williams, Barbara.
  Mitzi and the elephants.

  Summary: Mitzi becomes friends with the elephant
keeper at the zoo, from whom she hopes to learn how to
train big animals so she can get a Saint Bernard puppy.
  1. Children's stories, American. [1. Elephants—
Fiction. 2. Zoos—Fiction] I. McCully, Emily Arnold,
ill. II. Title.
PZ7.W65587Mg 1985 [Fic] 84-13743
ISBN 0-525-44158-1

Published in the United States by E. P. Dutton, Inc.,
2 Park Avenue, New York, N.Y. 10016

Published simultaneously in Canada by
Fitzhenry & Whiteside Limited, Toronto

Editor: Ann Durell   Designer: Edith T. Weinberg

Printed in the U.S.A.   COBE   First Edition
10 9 8 7 6 5 4 3 2 1

Acknowledgments

The episode in chapter 9 of this book is based upon a true incident reported by Dick Richards in *Life With Alice,* Coward, McCann, 1944.

The author also wishes to thank the following people for their generosity in providing factual material and actual incidents about elephants:

Gayle Cole, Coordinator of Youth Services, Stockton–San Joaquin County Public Library, Stockton, California

Alfred J. Perry, former Elephant Keeper, National Zoological Park, Washington, D.C.

Ed Roberts, P.A.K., former Senior Supervisor, Animal Division, The Stone Memorial Zoo, Stoneham, Massachusetts

for Ryan Sanders

Contents

1

Puppies and Popsicles

Three hundred dollars. Each of the puppies in that pen was worth three hundred dollars.

Mitzi had come to the kennel with her best friend, Elsie Wolf, to see the new litter. Elsie's uncle raised puppies worth three hundred dollars each. And he was going to give one to Elsie and one to Mitzi.

Just think. Her very own dog. Mitzi McAllister, who loved all animals and planned to be a biologist when she grew up, had never owned a pet. But now she was going to own a dog worth three hundred dollars.

Boy! Would that be something to tell the other kids when fourth grade started next month.

Mitzi poked her nose through the chain link fence. She longed to pick up one of the puppies

1

and cuddle it. But they were all too far away, pushing against their mother on the far side of the pen.

"Is your Uncle Jeff really going to give each of us a puppy?" Mitzi asked.

Elsie smiled, showing her dimples. "Yep." Then she stuck out her tongue and carefully licked her half of an orange Popsicle. It was almost to a point.

"How come?" Mitzi asked.

Elsie paused to suck on the end of the pointy Popsicle. Mitzi's half had been eaten a long time ago. But Elsie could make a Popsicle last forever. "He can't show the gray and white ones," Elsie said at last.

"Show?" asked Mitzi. How come Elsie's uncle hid the gray and white puppies?

"Uncle Jeff breeds the puppies for dog shows," Elsie explained. "But the gray ones never win ribbons. And there were two puppies in the litter that were gray and white instead of brown and white."

Hmmph, thought Mitzi. Judges at dog shows must be dumb. What difference did the color make?

Elsie gave her Popsicle another lick. "I like the gray ones better anyway."

One of the gray and white puppies had now left its mother's side and was stumbling toward the

fence. Mitzi poked the toe of her sneaker through the steel mesh to climb up the side of the pen.

"Don't do that," Elsie commanded.

"How come?" Mitzi asked.

"The mother might bite you."

Mitzi scowled. She was not afraid of dogs.

"Mother animals sometimes act mean when they have babies to protect," Elsie added.

Mitzi edged back from the pen. She had heard about mother animals acting mean when they had babies to protect. Especially mother bears and mother elephants. Somehow this mother in the pen reminded Mitzi of an elephant. It was the biggest dog she had ever seen.

"Uncle Jeff wanted to give me both of the gray and white puppies so they could live together," Elsie said. "Daddy didn't mind, but Mama wouldn't let us. So I told Uncle Jeff that he should give the other dog to you because we see each other nearly every day, and the puppies could play together."

Boy, thought Mitzi. Elsie Wolf *was* a wonderful best friend.

"I told him how much you love animals," Elsie said. "I told him you would feed your puppy real dog food. Not table scraps. And brush it. And walk it every day. And train it."

Mitzi nodded. Of course she would do all those things.

Elsie gave her Popsicle stick a long, final lick. Then she held it at arm's length between her thumb and index finger and dropped it into the garbage can near the pen. "And I told him your stepfather is a good carpenter who would love to build a fence around your yard. Uncle Jeff said you can't have the puppy unless you have a fence."

Mitzi swallowed. "How soon will we need a fence?" she croaked. Her voice sounded so funny she hardly recognized it.

"Not for three weeks," said Elsie. "The puppies are four weeks old now. But they can't leave their mother until they're seven weeks."

"Oh," said Mitzi.

"Three weeks will give Walter a long time to build a fence," Elsie said.

"Sure," said Mitzi. But she wasn't sure at all. Only last night she had heard Walter ask her mother not to expect any yard work from him for a while. His editor was angry because the manuscript for the biology textbook he was writing wasn't finished.

How would he feel about building a fence for a puppy in three weeks?

2

A Doggone Problem

Mitzi worried all the way home from the kennel. How would she ask Walter to build a fence when she knew how busy he was?

She waited to say anything until the family was seated at the dinner table and Walter had served himself some of Nana Potts' meatloaf Wellington.

"We need a pet," said Mitzi.

Three-year-old Darwin quit putting peas onto his spoon with his slobbery fingers and sat up straight. "Yeah. We need an alligator."

Eleven-year-old Frederick swirled a thick layer of ketchup on his meatloaf. "Why not? We already have a tyrannosaurus rex. We might as well get an alligator, too."

"Yeah, we can have fights," said Darwin. "I'm the meanest dinosaur who was ever born. I can

6

beat up an old alligator." He held up his hands like claws and made his favorite tyrannosaurus rex noise. "Grunch."

Nana Potts smiled sweetly at Darwin. "Dinosaurs need to eat so we'll be stronger than all the other animals. Let's eat our meatloaf, dear."

"Mmm," Walter muttered thickly. "It tastes great."

"It certainly does," said Mitzi's mother.

Why weren't the important people listening to Mitzi? "It's time I had a puppy," she informed them.

"It's time I had an alligator," said Darwin.

Darwin was ruining everything. Why didn't he shut up? "I'm eight and a half years old," Mitzi argued.

"I'm three and a half years old," Darwin echoed.

That was too much. "No one cares how old you are," Mitzi said.

"Yes they do," said Darwin, batting his eyelashes at his grandmother. Even though his hair was blond, Darwin had long, black eyelashes that strangers always noticed. "You care, don't you, Nana?" he said.

"Of course I care," said Nana Potts. "We're the sweetest three-year-old in the whole world."

Frederick rolled his eyes at the ceiling.

Nana Potts wasn't through talking. "We're so

sweet an alligator might try to eat us up." She patted Darwin's head. "A puppy is a much nicer pet for boys and girls."

Mitzi was encouraged by this unexpected support from Nana Potts. "No three-year-old can take care of an alligator," Mitzi said. "But Elsie Wolf's uncle knows that I'm big enough to take care of a dog. He raises puppies that cost three hundred dollars, and he's going to give me one."

Mitzi's mother choked, then took a sip of water. "Give you one?" she asked.

"What's the catch?" said Frederick.

Mitzi bit her lip, thinking hard. Buttering her baked potato, she waited for the tight feeling in her chest to go away. "Catch?" she repeated.

"No one gives away a dog worth three hundred dollars unless there's a catch," said Frederick. "There's a catch, isn't there?"

Mitzi set her buttery knife on the tablecloth. It was hard work to eat and explain things at the same time. Especially when Walter—the main person she was talking to—wouldn't look at her. "Well—" she began.

Frederick pinched up his lips and wiped them with a paper napkin. "I bet it's a Doberman pinscher that steals things. Like that stupid Rosie on University Street."

"It isn't a Doberman pinscher," said Mitzi.

"Then I bet it's a German shepherd that bites people," said Frederick. "All this neighborhood needs is a German shepherd that bites people."

"It isn't a German shepherd. And it doesn't bite people. It's just a puppy," said Mitzi.

"Well, what's the catch?" Frederick demanded.

Mitzi swallowed and looked hopefully in Walter's direction. "We have to build a fence. He won't give it to us until we build a fence."

"Of course not," said Nana Potts loudly.

Startled, Mitzi turned around. Was Nana Potts on her side or not? That lady was hard to figure out sometimes. Right now she was staring at Walter, her mouth set in a straight line.

"I knew there was a catch," said Frederick. "There's always a catch."

Mitzi's mother reached for her hand. "Your father has already missed the deadline for his manuscript, honey. He doesn't have time to build a fence."

"I'm sorry, Mitzi," said Walter.

"You'll have to tell Elsie's uncle we can't take a dog right now," said Mitzi's mother. "Maybe another time."

Mitzi yanked her hand away. "There may not be another time. He's only giving me the puppy because it's gray and white and he can't take it to dog shows. He may never have a gray and white one again. I'll never have another chance for a puppy worth three hundred dollars."

"Darling, the price of a puppy won't make you love it more," said Mitzi's mother. "The best pet

I ever had as a little girl was a mongrel we found on the highway."

"They sell stray dogs at the pound for twenty-five dollars," said Frederick.

"Maybe someone will give you an alligator worth three hundred dollars," Darwin suggested brightly.

"You ought to go to the pound someday and look at all the dogs who need homes," Frederick told his stepsister.

These darn old people wouldn't see her cry. Mitzi bit her lip to make her chin stop quivering.

"*Hmmph!*" said Nana Potts, waving in the air the big spoon from the bowl of peas. "Well, if the rest of you won't help us, Mitzi and I will build a fence ourselves."

Mitzi stopped biting her lip, and her mouth fell open. Nana Potts *was* on her side. Good old Nana Potts!

"Mom, you and Mitzi can't build a fence," said Walter. "Do you know how much chain link weighs? Especially if you build a strong six-foot fence. And you have to set the posts in concrete."

Nana Potts lowered the spoon slightly. "Who says we need a six-foot fence for a little puppy? We'll build a shorter one."

"Well," said Mitzi's mother. "Maybe I could help, too." Turning to Mitzi, she said, "What kind of a puppy is it, honey?"

"A Saint Bernard," said Mitzi.

"A Saint Bernard!" cried Mitzi's mother.

"A Saint Bernard!" cried Walter.

"What's a Saint Bernard?" said Darwin.

"A Saint Bernard is the biggest dog in the world," said Mitzi's mother.

Frederick tipped his head backwards and stared at the ceiling, the way he always did when he was about to make a speech. "Saint Bernards were developed by monks in the Swiss Alps to help them rescue travelers lost in the snow. They are intelligent and friendly dogs that are especially gentle with children. But the puppies grow very rapidly, sometimes reaching a size of two hundred and twenty pounds by their second year. That is about as much as Patricia and Nana weigh together."

Holding up his hands like claws, Darwin bared little white teeth. "Grunch! I'm not afraid of a Saint Bernard."

"You don't need to be," said know-it-all Frederick. "We'll never have one. Nana and Patricia can't build a big enough fence to hold one."

Walter nodded in agreement. "A Saint Bernard will need an eight-foot fence of the heaviest weight chain link. There's no way that you and Patricia could build a fence like that without help, Mom."

Nana Potts put her tablespoon down with a chesty sigh.

Mitzi threw her fork on her plate. There! That

would show Walter what she thought of his old textbook. A father should think of other things besides his work sometimes. A father should think of his new little girl.

She pushed her chair away from the table, ran up the stairs to her bedroom two at a time, and slammed the door shut. For good measure, she kicked it, too. There! *Now* what was Walter thinking?

Poor Mitzi, that's what he was thinking. Poor Mitzi is upstairs crying her eyes out because I'm too mean to build a fence for her puppy.

Maybe she really should cry. Maybe she should go downstairs in a little while with her face all tear-stained and blotchy.

She threw herself on her bed and tried to cry. No tears.

She sniffled and heaved her chest up and down. No tears.

She pinched her arm as hard as she could until it really hurt. No tears.

Phooey.

She sat up again. Maybe she was too old to cry. Maybe eight-and-a-half-year-olds were big enough to solve their problems other ways. But how?

She sat there a long time, biting her lip and thinking.

No ideas came.

Well, at least she didn't have to solve her problem today. Walking over to her desk, she took her calendar from the wall.

Today was Wednesday, August 10. Three weeks from today would be Wednesday, August 31.

With a black felt-tipped pen, she put a big *X* through the *10*. It was comforting to know that she still had twenty-one more days to figure something out.

3

A Trip to the Zoo

Mitzi felt torn.

She wanted to go to the zoo, and she didn't want to go to the zoo.

Of course she wanted to see the animals. But she didn't want to go to the zoo with Walter. *He* should stay home.

If Walter was too busy to build a fence, how come he had time to go talk to the zoo director? If Walter was too busy to build a fence, how come he had time to plan ways to raise money for the zoo? If Walter was too busy to build a fence, how come he had time to be on television tonight?

Walter had no business going anywhere.

Besides, his dumb idea wouldn't work. He couldn't change Mitzi's mind. No one could change Mitzi's mind. She wanted her Saint Bernard puppy.

Through the bathroom wall, she had overheard her parents talking in their bedroom. Walter thought that Mitzi should watch the zookeepers work while he was talking to Dr. Harmer. Then she would see how hard it is to care for big animals. Mitzi would decide she wanted a small dog, like a poodle. Or better still, a kitten.

HAH!

Still, a trip to the zoo *was* a trip to the zoo. And Walter wasn't apt to stay home just because Mitzi wouldn't go with him. He was already in the car, honking for her.

Grimly she put an X through the *11* on her calendar, walked downstairs and outside, and climbed into the back of the car with Frederick and Darwin. Darwin had removed the clunky blue swim fins that he called tyrannosaurus rex feet. But he was still wearing Nana Potts' slitty sunglasses that he thought looked like dinosaur eyes. Frederick was wearing a green T-shirt with letters that said SUPPORT YOUR LOCAL ZOO. Mitzi sighed. Brothers could be very embarrassing.

Arriving at the zoo before it was open to the public, they drove through a gate marked Employees Only. Walter parked the car and turned around in his seat for a last-minute lecture. Mitzi and Darwin must do everything Frederick told them. And Frederick must watch his brother and sister carefully. Then they all climbed out, and

Walter headed off alone toward a brick building with a sign that said Office.

Frederick nodded toward a building down the path. "That's the monkey house. Let's go there first."

"Nope," said Darwin. "The mean Tyrannosaurus Rex wants to see the alligators." He stuck his left index finger in his mouth and sucked hungrily.

"But the alligator house is way across the zoo," Frederick explained, pointing. "Way over there. I don't want to take you that far."

Darwin removed his finger from his mouth. "Okay," he chirped. "I'll take myself." He started running in the direction Frederick had pointed. "Good-bye," he called over his shoulder.

Frederick ran after him and grabbed his brother by the back of the shirt. Nana Potts' green sunglasses slid down Darwin's little nose. His curly blond hair stuck out in every direction. He looked more like a clown than a dinosaur.

"Dad told me to watch you," Frederick said.

Darwin grinned cheerfully at his brother. "Okay. Watch me at the alligator house." He squirmed out of Frederick's grasp and darted off again.

Frederick shrugged. "Come on, Mitzi. We won't have any peace until he's seen his alligators."

Darwin had won. There was no need for him to run anymore. He slowed up and walked alongside Frederick and Mitzi, playing Tyrannosaurus Rex. Curling up his hands like claws, he twisted his mouth into a snarl. "Grunch!" he told the two elephants being led outdoors by their keeper.

The elephants were not afraid of dinosaurs. They ignored Darwin. Instead, they pushed and butted against each other. They paid no attention to the long stick their keeper was poking at them or the swear words he was shouting.

They're fighting, Mitzi told herself. Those two elephants are fighting, and their keeper can't control them.

Then, suddenly, they stopped. Both elephants raised their trunks in the air, waving and trumpeting. Another keeper was walking toward them from a different direction.

The elephants were waving to that man. No, that wasn't possible. Elephants didn't wave to people. Or did they? The man was waving and calling, too.

SMACK! Mitzi felt a sharp sting on her side. She turned to see Darwin scowling at her.

"Come *on*," he said. "I want to see the alligators."

Mitzi scowled back. "I want to watch the elephants."

Darwin stamped his foot. "You can't. Frederick promised I could see the alligators first."

18

Frederick had not promised. Mitzi had heard the whole conversation. She looked toward Frederick, hoping he would repeat it for Darwin. But he was staring in the opposite direction, pretending he didn't know his brother or sister. Mitzi drew herself up tall. "Elephants are more interesting," she told Darwin.

"Alligators are meaner," said Darwin. "I like mean animals."

Sighing, Frederick folded his arms across his chest. "You two will have to decide. I can't watch both of you in different places."

Mitzi made a face. She did not need to be watched. She was eight years old. "You take Darwin to the alligator house. I'll stay here and wait for you."

"*Yeah!*" said Darwin.

Frederick thought about it. "Will you promise to stay right here? Not go anywhere? With anyone?"

Why should Mitzi want to go anywhere when she could stay right here and watch the elephants? "I promise," she said.

"Okay," Frederick said. "Come on, Darwin."

While Mitzi had been arguing with Darwin, the second zookeeper had stopped a few feet from her. He was talking to the elephants across the thick stone wall and shallow moat that kept the zoo visitors safe. Despite the distance that separated the elephants and the keeper, their trunks reached out to him, touching his arms.

He was a short man about the same age as Mitzi's mother. He had long sandy hair almost to his shoulders. A beard and moustache covered his mouth.

"Well there, Daisy," he said to the bigger of the two elephants. "Are you going to play me a tune this morning?"

A tune? Mitzi edged closer.

The man pulled a giant harmonica from the pocket of his blue coveralls and held it out toward the elephant. She snatched it with a strange-looking "finger" at the end of her trunk and held it in place.

Mitzi stared. Was this elephant really going to play a harmonica?

Yes. Daisy blew. *Whumm.*

Then she returned the harmonica to the man. She seemed very pleased with herself.

"Fantastic," he said. "We're talking Elton John." He reached into his pocket again and unwrapped a granola bar. One of those big ones with peanut butter.

Mitzi's mouth watered.

The smaller elephant bumped against Daisy's side and tried to reach the granola. But the keeper handed it to Daisy. Daisy bolted it into her mouth.

The smaller elephant trumpeted.

"Take it easy, Cupcake. I brought you a present, too. But first you'll have to play me a song."

Cupcake held out her trunk and swayed impatiently back and forth.

"Knock it off, Porter." The first zookeeper was scowling at the second man. "Don't you have any work to do?"

"Not for five minutes," said the second man. "I don't have to report for five minutes." He winked at Mitzi. Then he handed the harmonica to the smaller elephant.

Cupcake raised her trunk high in the air. *Whummmmmmm.*

"Out of this world," said the second keeper. He turned to Mitzi with another wink. "A regular star."

Mitzi nodded. She'd never heard of elephants that could play the harmonica before.

Cupcake waved her trunk excitedly.

"I told you, Porter," said the first keeper. "Move on."

"Listen, man," said the second keeper, "you don't let number one on the charts go unrewarded." From another pocket, he took a package of Hostess cupcakes and unwrapped them for the elephant.

Cupcake snatched them one at a time and tossed them into her mouth.

"Okay, Porter. The fun's over. Shove off."

The second keeper didn't answer but stood still while Cupcake stroked his shoulder and cheek with the tip of her trunk. At last he backed away, waving first to Mitzi and then to the elephants. "See you later," he told the elephants. And he headed off down the path to the left.

Immediately, Mitzi heard Darwin's footsteps and turned. He was racing toward her with Frederick behind.

"You sure weren't gone very long," Mitzi said. "Weren't the alligators mean enough?"

"The alligator house is locked," Darwin said with a frown. He turned toward the keeper inside the moat with Daisy and Cupcake. "Will you open the alligator house for us?"

"The zoo isn't open yet," grumbled the man. "You kids don't belong here. Get out."

Darwin was indignant. "We don't have to. We were invited."

The man seemed doubtful. "By who?"

Frederick spoke from between closed teeth. "Let's go, Darwin."

"By your boss," Darwin told the man. "So you better open the alligator house for us."

"That isn't my job," said the man.

Frederick looked pained.

"You better open it," said Darwin. "Or we'll tell your boss that you're lazy."

The man muttered something under his breath. At once, Cupcake lifted her trunk and whomped Daisy.

The man poked Cupcake with his long stick and said a dirty word.

"And we'll tell your boss that you beat the elephants and say naughty words," said Darwin.

Grabbing his brother by the arm, Frederick started down the path. "Come on, you turkey."

When they reached the zoo office, Walter was standing outside the door with another man. Walter looked up with a smile and introduced the children to Dr. Harmer, the director of the zoo.

Dr. Harmer broke into a grin as he read the words on Frederick's shirt. "Support Your Local Zoo. That's a nice T-shirt you've got on, Frederick. Why don't you come on television tonight with your father and me and wear that shirt?"

"Tonight is my chess club," Frederick said. "But Nana could wash this shirt so Mitzi could wear it. It wouldn't be much too big for her. Anyway, Mitzi is the one who should be on television with you. She's planning to be a biologist when she grows up."

"Okay," said Dr. Harmer with a shrug. He turned to Walter. "Bring Mitzi along when you come to the studio tonight."

Mitzi grinned. She could hardly wait to tell Elsie Wolf.

"I want to be on television, too," said Darwin.

Walter patted Darwin on the head. "Maybe

some other time, pal. When you're a little older."

"I am a little older," said Darwin. "I'm a little older than I was yesterday."

"Oh, the younger the better," said Dr. Harmer. "They won't be on camera long. And audiences always enjoy seeing cute children."

Mitzi wasn't so sure. Even if he was only on camera a few minutes, Darwin the Terrible Tyrannosaurus Rex would find some way to mess things up.

4

The TV Sit Comedy

"Where's the green room?" Mitzi asked.

Mitzi was an expert on green rooms. When her parents weren't home, Nana Potts let Mitzi stay up late to watch "The Tonight Show." Green rooms were where the guests waited.

"Green room?" repeated the man. Then his face relaxed into a smile. "I'm afraid we don't have a green room. This is educational TV. We're pretty low budget around here."

"Well, where do we sit down?" she asked.

"Over there," said the man, nodding toward some folding chairs against the wall. "Take your brother over there. I'll come get you when it's time for you to be on camera."

"I want to be on camera now," said Darwin.

"Well, the program hasn't started yet," said the

man cheerfully. "Besides, we're saving the best part until last. First the Issues Man will talk to your father and Dr. Harmer. Then a zookeeper is bringing a zebra to be on camera. And then I'll come get you."

"What are we supposed to say?" asked Mitzi.

"Don't worry about it. The Issues Man will ask you some questions about zoos and why you like to go there. Just answer him naturally."

Boy, thought Mitzi. Answering naturally was something you should never let Darwin do. Especially on television. She wondered if she should warn the man. Oh well. She shrugged and looked around the room.

It was a big, high-ceilinged room that reminded her of the multipurpose room at school. The difference was that the multipurpose room had nice shiny wood on the floor. And a genuine stage at one end. This TV studio had a crummy floor and two make-believe stages. Just little platforms with narrow steps leading up to them. Her father, Dr. Harmer, and the Issues Man now sat on blue sofas on one of the platforms. Two photographers were pushing big cameras around to study the men from different sides.

Here was the thing Mitzi could hardly believe. The studio didn't even have seats for the audience. Just three dumb folding chairs against the wall. What would Johnny Carson's audience do if they had to sit on dumb chairs like these?

Darwin tugged on the man's pant leg. "Do all of us go up there where Daddy is?"

"Yes," said the man.

Darwin tugged on the man's pants again. "It won't work."

"What won't work?" he asked.

"A zebra can't climb those steps," Darwin said.

The man hit his forehead with the end of his fist. "Oh my gosh!" He ran toward the door, calling back to Mitzi and Darwin over his shoulder. "Go sit on those chairs. Stay there. Hear? And don't get in the way of the cameras."

Hmmph. As if Mitzi didn't know better than to get in the way of the cameras! Darwin, of course, might do anything, though. Her mother had been married to Darwin's father for two months, but Mitzi still hadn't figured Darwin out. Sometimes he really did seem like a genius, like everyone said he was. He realized that a zebra couldn't climb those steps, when even the grown-ups didn't notice. But sometimes he did such dumb things, he made her want to scream.

Like right now.

Darwin ran to the folding chairs and sprawled on his stomach, stretching out his arms and legs on all three of them. There was no room for Mitzi to sit down.

"Get up," she told him.

"I'm asleep," Darwin said.

"Then you won't mind if I sit on you," Mitzi said. She bent her knees slowly, testing his reaction.

Darwin scrambled to his feet and ducked under a chair. "This is my dinosaur cave. Don't come in it or I'll eat you up."

Mitzi sat primly on a chair. She had no intention of crawling on that filthy floor. She might get her new skirt dirty.

Mitzi had wanted to wear a dress on television. The frilly white one she had worn to her mother's wedding. But Walter said no. She must wear Frederick's yucky green T-shirt with letters that said SUPPORT YOUR LOCAL ZOO. So they had compromised. To go with the T-shirt, her mother had bought her a new green-and-brown plaid skirt with pleats all the way around.

With her hand, she smoothed the pleats of her new skirt, knowing how nice she looked. She certainly wouldn't crawl under a chair and get it dirty. Especially before she was to appear on television. Everyone would be watching the program. Her mother. Nana Potts. Elsie Wolf. Even Mr. Ledgard, the janitor from school. (Elsie had promised to call him.)

A noise from the doorway interrupted Mitzi's thoughts. The man with the button in his ear was shouting to four other men carrying a huge plank.

"Set it up on that side. Away from the cameras."

The men did as they were told. There. A ramp for the zebra to climb to the platform.

Darwin sprang to his feet and put his hands on his hips. "Well," he hollered to the man with the button in his ear. "That's better, you dummy."

Mitzi wondered if she should scold Darwin first for his bad manners or for the dirt on his pants and arms. But before she could decide, a man came in the door. He was leading a zebra with a rope.

It was Mitzi's friend from this morning. The zookeeper with the harmonica.

Beaming, Mitzi waved to him. "Hi."

The keeper came closer, looking puzzled. He didn't seem to be quite sure who Mitzi was.

"I'm Mitzi McAllister," she told him. "I was the girl at the zoo this morning. Remember? I saw you help Daisy and Cupcake play the harmonica."

A smile brightened the keeper's face like colored lights on a Christmas tree. "Oh . . . yeah. Glad to meet you, Mitzi. I'm Ed Porter. Call me Ed."

"My name is Charles Darwin Potts," said the Tyrannosaurus Rex. "But you can call me Darwin. I live at 1425 Sigsbee Avenue. My phone number is 581–6272. I'm three and a half years old. I'm a genius who invents things. I'm going to win the Nobel prize for inventions when I grow up."

"Listen, I've never met a Nobel prize winner before," said Ed. He turned to Mitzi. "Are you a genius, too?"

"No," she said slowly. Of course, her third-grade teacher *had* promoted her to the best reading group last year. Maybe she should mention that. Deciding not to, she said, "I'm going to be a biologist when I grow up. I . . . I want to train big animals. Like Saint Bernards. Can you teach me?"

Ed shook his head, licking the end of his moustache. "Man, I don't know anything about Saint Bernards."

Mitzi's disappointment must have shown on her face because Ed spoke again. "Listen, Saint Bernards are smart animals, too. Just like elephants. I bet you'd train them the same way you train elephants. If you'd like to meet me sometime at the zoo . . ."

"When?" said Mitzi.

Suddenly the zebra jerked his head, and Ed grabbed the rope tighter. "Easy, Romeo. Easy. You're all right, man."

"When?" Mitzi repeated.

Ed kept his eyes on the zebra. "Listen, Romeo. A few television lights won't hurt you. Anyway, we're only talking two minutes. Three at the most. There's nothing to worry about."

"When?" Mitzi asked for a third time.

31

"Uh," said Ed, looking up. "Can you get up real early?"

"Sure," Mitzi said.

"I always get up early," said Darwin. "So I can wake Mitzi up."

Ed smiled his bright smile. "Well, get her up in time to meet me at seven-thirty tomorrow." He turned to Mitzi. "I can show you how I train the elephants before I have to report to the zebra and giraffe area at eight o'clock."

The man with the button in his ear walked over and spoke to Ed. "It's time for the zebra now. Start leading him toward the ramp."

"Meet me at the employees' entrance at seven-thirty," Ed told Mitzi. He yanked at the zebra's rope.

Grinning to herself, Mitzi watched Ed lead the zebra toward the ramp. Boy. She was going to learn how to train a Saint Bernard, just the way Elsie had promised her uncle that Mitzi would do. The puppy was practically hers. Now all she had to do was persuade Walter to build a fence.

Suddenly the zebra stopped. Maybe it was the cameras. Maybe it was the lights. Maybe it was the ramp. But Romeo acted scared. He jerked his big head and tried to pull free from the rope.

The man with the button in his ear raced over to help Ed, but it took both men to hold the animal still.

Then it happened. The terrible, terrible thing happened.

"Look," said Darwin with a giggle. "Romeo is going wee-wee."

Wee-wee was too dainty a word for what Romeo was doing. Water was pouring out of him like rain from a downspout. All over the floor. All over Ed's boots. All over the shiny black shoes of the man with the button in his ear.

The man motioned frantically to Mitzi and Darwin. "We'll never get this zebra up the ramp. You kids go instead."

Mitzi stood up first, picking her way carefully around the huge puddle on the floor. Worried about getting her shoes wet and about what she would say on the television program, she didn't notice Darwin running up behind her.

Darwin bumped into her, and Mitzi's foot slipped. Before you could say "black and white zebra," Mitzi was sitting on the floor. In the middle of the yellow puddle.

YUCK!

She sprang quickly to her feet, but it was too late. Her shoes were wet. Her new plaid skirt was wet. Even Frederick's SUPPORT YOUR LOCAL ZOO T-shirt was wet.

Mitzi was furious. She couldn't appear on television looking like this.

She wanted to scream. She wanted to run after

Darwin, grab him by the back of his shirt, and push *him* down in the yellow yuck. But it was too late. He was already walking up the wooden ramp, headed toward the blue sofas behind the television lights.

Above Mitzi's head was a television monitor. She could see for herself the program that was being broadcast into living rooms all over Kansas.

"Isn't your sister with you?" asked the Issues Man.

"Nope," Darwin chirped. "Mitzi just fell down and wet her pants."

5

The Fight

The next morning, Mitzi tried very, very hard to put what had happened at the TV studio out of her mind. When she thought about it, she wanted to cry or to scream or to shake Darwin so hard his curly blond hair went straight. Getting up at six o'clock helped. She was too sleepy to do much thinking.

Nana Potts helped, too. She woke Mitzi with a hug and a kiss. And she packed her breakfast when Mitzi said she wasn't hungry. She put oranges, bananas, and Mitzi's favorite bran and pecan muffins in a lunch bucket.

"You'll be hungry before your mother comes back to pick you up at nine-thirty," she said.

Ed met Mitzi at the gate. They walked together to the elephant area.

"Do you always come to work this early?" she asked. She tried not to yawn.

"I do if I want to see the elephants," said Ed.

"But you see the elephants all day," Mitzi argued.

"Man, I wish I did. There are two elephant keepers, but I'm not one of them," Ed explained. "I work in the zebra and giraffe area."

"But . . . but . . ." Mitzi sputtered. "You should be working with the elephants."

Ed shrugged. "Tell it to Charlie. Or Harmer."

Harmer was *Dr.* Harmer. Mitzi could figure that out. "Is Charlie the man who was yelling at you yesterday?" she asked.

"No, that was Pete," said Ed. "Pete and Charlie are the two elephant keepers. Charlie is the main one. He's the man I applied to four years ago. But he gave the job to Pete. Charlie is Pete's uncle."

Oh. Now Mitzi understood. Just because Elsie Wolf had a nice uncle who was going to give Mitzi a puppy didn't mean that all uncles were nice. Sometimes uncles were unfair. Like Mitzi's swimming teacher who chose his niece to do the back dive for the parents' program. No one had to tell Mitzi about uncles.

"Maybe you should ask Dr. Harmer," Mitzi suggested.

"You don't think I have?" asked Ed. "Man, we're talking three and four applications every year. For nearly four years. Listen, I'd do almost anything to be able to work in the elephant area."

"I bet Cupcake and Daisy don't pet Pete with their trunks the way they pet you," said Mitzi. "And I bet they don't play the harmonica for him. Dr. Harmer should be smart enough to see that."

"No, but Charlie and Harmer don't know about all that. They're only around from nine to five. Pete and I are assistant keepers, so we have to work a split shift. We come early and stay late but get time off in the afternoon. And I train the elephants before the zoo opens and after it closes," Ed explained.

Mitzi bit her lip. Maybe she could think of some way to help Ed. When she wasn't busy thinking about some way to get Walter to build a fence for her puppy.

"Anyhow," Ed continued, "Harmer's got other things to worry about besides the animals. Budgets. And fund-raising projects. And keeping the public happy. I sure wouldn't want his job. Just give me the animals. Especially the elephants. Man, they're wonderful, those elephants. Smart. And loyal. Once they accept you, they're the best friends you'll ever have in the world. Of course, they like to play tricks on you, too. They have a great sense of humor."

Mitzi wasn't sure she'd want a great big animal

like an elephant playing tricks on her. "What kind of tricks?" she asked.

Ed's words came out in a rush. He seemed to be happy to talk to someone about elephants. "Take Daisy, for instance. Once when I was hosing down the elephant house—I know that isn't my job, but sometimes I do it anyway—the water stopped. I checked on the problem. And there was Daisy standing on the hose. She had shut off the water completely. I yelled at her, and she raised her foot. Then she made this funny little noise, and I knew she was laughing at me. After that, she pulled the same stunt lots of times. And she caught me by surprise every time."

"How about Cupcake?" Mitzi asked. "Does she play tricks, too?"

"Not really," said Ed. "She has a different personality. Cupcake likes attention. She likes to have her tongue rubbed. And if you're good to her, she'll pat you back with her trunk. She's only nine years old. She still isn't full grown. But she was just a baby when I started working here. She used to follow me around like a puppy."

Mitzi smiled to herself, thinking of the Saint Bernard puppy she hoped to own.

"But when Cupcake grew older, she got jealous," Ed continued. "She couldn't stand it if Daisy got more attention than she did. Or better food. She'd throw fits and take out her anger on

Daisy. Man, we're talking *elephant* fits. Sometimes I think Pete ignores Cupcake on purpose just to see what she'll do. Cupcake is always butting Daisy with her tusks."

"How come Daisy doesn't butt her back?" Mitzi asked. "Daisy is bigger."

"Yeah, but Daisy is an Asian elephant. She doesn't have tusks. As a rule, only male Asians have tusks. Not many female Asians have them. Cupcake is an African elephant. Anyhow, Daisy is a pretty mellow lady most of the time. She doesn't get excited the way Cupcake does. And she's patient with Cupcake because she knows Cupcake is still a baby."

For a man who wasn't even their real keeper, Ed certainly knew a lot about Daisy and Cupcake. He was talking about them almost as if they were people. "Dr. Harmer should let you be the elephant keeper," Mitzi told him. "It isn't fair that Pete gets to do it just because Charlie is his uncle."

Ed shook his head. "Listen, Mitzi. You better get used to something. Life isn't always fair."

Well, life should be fair! If Mitzi were in charge of the world, she'd see to it that people got what they deserved. And elephants, too.

"Daisy and Cupcake should have something to say about it," Mitzi argued. "I can tell that they want you."

"Harmer doesn't have time to worry about what the animals want," said Ed. "He has to keep the money coming in so the zoo can open every day. That means keeping the public happy. And lots of important people are Pete's and Charlie's friends."

"Well, you have important friends, too," said Mitzi.

"Like who?" asked Ed.

"Like me," said Mitzi.

She meant it, too. She was Ed's friend. Making friends was the one good thing that had happened at the television studio last night.

Ed stopped walking and put his hand on Mitzi's shoulder, looking at her with deep brown eyes. "I appreciate it."

Suddenly there was a trumpeting noise and a loud *crack* from the elephant area. A few seconds later, they saw Pete running from the elephant house toward Dr. Harmer's office.

"Man, that sounds like real trouble," cried Ed. "I'll have to go and try to calm those elephants down." He ran toward the gate of the elephant wall.

Clutching her lunch bucket, Mitzi trotted behind Ed and saw him open the locked gate at the side of the thick wall. He picked up a long stick inside the wall and crept toward the elephants.

Cupcake sensed his presence. Without turning around, she raised her trunk, sniffing the air.

Seizing her advantage, Daisy whopped the smaller elephant with her trunk, like a mother spanking a naughty child.

"Stop that, Daisy!" yelled Ed. The larger elephant lowered the trunk that she had raised for a second spanking.

Now Cupcake had the advantage. She lowered her head as if to ram Daisy with her tusks.

"You, too, Cupcake," cried Ed. He caught the smaller elephant's trunk with the hook on the end of his stick. She stopped moving her head, as if the hook hurt.

"Look what you've done, Cupcake," said Ed. "You've broken your tusk. Listen, you girls better learn some manners. Cut out all this rough stuff. You know what I mean?"

Mitzi grinned. Ed really did treat these elephants as if they were people. As if he were their father.

Footsteps sounded from Mitzi's left. She turned to see Pete and Dr. Harmer running toward the elephant gate.

"Well," said Dr. Harmer between heavy breaths. "Those elephants don't seem out of control to me."

"You should have seen them a minute ago," said Pete. "Cupcake broke her tusk against Daisy's side."

Mitzi stood up straight. "Well, Ed calmed them down," she reported. "I saw the whole thing. He's the only one who could do it."

Pete glared at Mitzi.

Dr. Harmer wiped the perspiration from his forehead with the back of his hand. In doing so, his wrist brushed against some long hairs that were hanging over one ear. Carefully he stretched them out and smoothed them over the bald spot on his head.

"Well, Pete, you *have* been having lots of trouble here lately. Maybe we should try Ed out in the elephant area for a while. I think I'll transfer you to the zebra and giraffe area for a couple of weeks, Pete, and we'll see how things go. We'll make the transfer immediately. You stay here for the rest of the day, Ed."

Across the thick wall that separated them, Mitzi and Ed shared a smile. Mitzi had helped Ed get the job he wanted. Now he was going to teach her how to train big animals so she could get the Saint Bernard puppy she wanted.

With a friendship like that, what could possibly go wrong?

6

The Elephant Protector

Pete shuffled off, his hands jammed deep in the pockets of his blue coveralls. But a few feet down the path, he paused to look sideways at Mitzi.

Mitzi shivered. What was Pete thinking? Was he planning to hurt her? No, of course not. That was silly.

Still, he looked pretty mean.

Dr. Harmer cleared his throat. He was frowning at his watch. "I'll talk to the vet about that broken tusk and the wound on Daisy's side, Ed. You get the elephant house cleaned up and try to get these animals calmed down before the zoo opens. We can't have them fighting when visitors arrive. Remember, I'm just trying you out in the elephant area for a couple of weeks."

Mitzi was left alone with Ed, Daisy, and Cupcake. She was still carrying her lunch bucket. She wondered where she could put it down. Nana Potts had been wrong. She was not hungry.

"Want a bran and pecan muffin?" she asked Ed.

"Sure," he said.

Mitzi opened the lunch box.

There were no bran and pecan muffins inside. There were no bananas or oranges. There was nothing at all to eat—just a pair of shiny, flat-heeled shoes.

Ed laughed. "I think I'll pass on the pecan muffins."

"Oh, I brought the wrong one," wailed Mitzi. "I brought Nana Potts' lunch box."

"Your grandma eats shoes?" Ed joked.

Mitzi saw nothing funny. "Nana Potts gave me *her* lunch bucket—the one she carries her dancing shoes in. It was supposed to be Frederick's, but he thinks he's too grown-up to use it."

"Want me to put it in the keepers' room for you?" Ed asked.

"I can do it," said Mitzi. "Open the gate for me."

Ed licked his moustache. "Listen, Mitzi. I don't think you should come inside the wall today. These girls are a bit high-strung, if you know what I mean."

Another disappointment. Mitzi wasn't going to be given a special lesson in training animals, after all. She was just going to stand outside the wall around the elephant area, like any zoo visitor.

"Daisy and Cupcake won't hurt me when you're there," she said.

"I know that," said Ed. "But I'm just on trial, remember. I can't afford to let these girls get noisy. And they've been acting pretty wild this morning. Man, we're talking broken tusks."

Mitzi sighed and handed the lunch bucket to Ed.

When he returned from taking it to the keepers' room, he groomed the animals near the wall so Mitzi could watch. One at a time, he hosed them down. Then he told Daisy to lie down on her side, and he brushed the back of her head.

"She sure doesn't have much hair," Mitzi said. "How come you have to brush it?"

"It relaxes her. Besides, Daisy likes to be pretty. Don't you, old girl?" said Ed.

Daisy waved her trunk in the air.

"How come you know so much about elephants?" Mitzi asked.

"I'll tell you something, Mitzi. There are two kinds of people in this world. People who understand elephants. And people who don't understand elephants."

As he brushed, Ed explained how he first realized he understood elephants. He was passing the elephant area when Daisy made a funny gurgling

47

noise. Ed felt sure she was asking for something. But she was standing near a bale of hay, so she wasn't asking for food. He checked the water trough, and sure enough, someone had turned off the hose. Daisy was asking for water.

From then on, Ed came every day to the elephant area, working with Daisy and Cupcake before he had to report to his own job. Soon Cupcake was following him like a shadow. And within a year, he had taught both elephants to respond to fifteen different commands.

"Do you think I could teach the elephants a command?" said Mitzi.

"Why not?" said Ed. "I mean you could if you're patient."

Of course Mitzi was patient. Who else would give the tooth fairy a second chance when she forgot to come the first night?

"My son Gary is eleven, not much older than you. He taught Daisy to kneel this summer," Ed explained.

"How?" Mitzi asked.

"Well, for a couple of weeks he didn't do anything," said Ed, who was now brushing Cupcake's hair. "He just came inside the elephant area and stayed by my side while I worked."

A couple of weeks? Of doing nothing? Mitzi stuck out her lower lip and blew the bangs off her forehead.

"Then, when I was sure the elephants accepted him, I let him hose Daisy down. Daisy is more even-tempered than Cupcake, so I let him start with Daisy," said Ed.

Whooey, thought Mitzi. Did it take this long to train a Saint Bernard? She shifted her weight to her other foot. "But how did Gary teach Daisy to kneel?"

"Well, first he knelt himself to show Daisy what he wanted," said Ed. "Then he said 'kneel' and held out a head of cabbage. Cupcake here doesn't like cabbage, but Daisy is wild about it."

"If Cupcake doesn't like cabbage, what did Gary use to teach *her* to kneel?" Mitzi asked.

"Cupcake hasn't learned to kneel yet. But we'll probably train her with cupcakes. Not all animals like cake. But this little lady flips over them. Don't you, girl?"

Worry crossed Ed's face. "Listen, Mitzi. Don't look now, but Pete is standing over there staring at us."

Much as she tried not to look, Mitzi couldn't resist a peek out of the corner of one eye. Sure enough. Pete was watching them from behind the popcorn stand.

"I better get inside the elephant house and start cleaning it," said Ed. "You can stay here and watch the elephants until your mother comes back to take you home." He started toward the door.

What a waste this morning had been. Mitzi had learned nothing at all.

Furthermore, the zoo had opened, and visitors were trickling down the paths. Two boys stopped outside the elephant area, just a few feet from Mitzi.

"Hey," one of them called to Ed, who had nearly reached the door. "How did that elephant break his tusk?"

Ed shrugged. "Beats me. I wasn't here." He disappeared into the building.

Mitzi, who did not care for the way grown-ups sometimes bent the truth, set matters straight. "She's a girl," Mitzi informed the boys. "And her name is Cupcake. And she broke her tusk fighting with the other elephant. Before Ed was her keeper, Cupcake used to fight with Daisy."

"Cupcake!" hooted the second boy. "That's a dumb name for an elephant."

"It is not," said Mitzi. "It's a perfect name for her. Some animals don't like cake. But Cupcake flips over it. I saw her eat some Hostess cupcakes yesterday."

"No kidding," said the second boy. He reached into a lunch bag he was carrying and pulled out a package of Hostess cupcakes. "I just happen to have some here." He punched the first boy with an elbow. "Want to see an elephant flip?"

The sign posted in front of them said Do Not

Feed The Animals. But Mitzi felt no need to mention it. After all, Ed had given the elephants treats yesterday. And Gary had used cabbage to teach Daisy to kneel.

Whiss went the paper from the package. Cupcake lifted her trunk in the air and sniffed.

"Okay, Cupcake. Flip," ordered the second boy. He held the cake toward the elephant. But just as Cupcake reached for it across the thick wall, he snatched it away.

The two boys bumped each other's shoulders, giggling.

"Come on, Cupcake. Let's see you flip," said the first boy.

"Flip, dummy," said the second boy. He held the cake about three inches from Cupcake's outstretched trunk, waving it back and forth.

Cupcake followed the moving cake with the tip of her trunk, her eyes growing angry.

Deep inside, Mitzi knew the boys were mostly teasing *her*. They were making fun of Mitzi for saying that an elephant could flip. But they were also teasing an animal. And that wasn't nice.

She planted both feet firmly on the ground, clenched her hands into mallets, and stood up so tall she nearly reached the second boy's chin. "Stop teasing that elephant," Mitzi demanded.

"Who's going to make me?" said the boy.

"I am," said Mitzi.

51

"You and who else?" said the boy.

Mitzi bit her lip. Just who could help her? Ed was inside the elephant house and wouldn't hear her call.

"I don't need anyone else," said Mitzi.

"You pea brain," said the boy.

Mitzi was not a pea brain. Without caring that she was just one eight-year-old girl against two boys who must be at least thirteen, she kicked the second boy in the shins.

"You bully," she cried. Mitzi seized the cake and handed it to Cupcake, who tossed it into her mouth.

"Hey!" yelled the boy.

He hadn't noticed that the other little cake had fallen from the package and was lying at his feet. Mitzi quickly snatched it and handed that one to Cupcake, too. Cupcake put the second cake into her mouth and swayed back and forth, acting pleased.

Recovered from the kick, the boy shoved Mitzi against the wall and kneed her in the stomach. "See how that feels, pea brain."

It felt terrible. Really terrible. But Mitzi wouldn't cry. She wouldn't.

Then he raised his fist as if to hit her face, but the first boy grabbed his arm. "Okay, she's learned her lesson. Let's go see the penguins."

Leaning against the wall, Mitzi watched the

boys walk away. Suddenly she felt her mother rubbing her cheek, the way she always did when Mitzi was sick or unhappy.

But it wasn't her mother. It was Cupcake rubbing Mitzi's cheek with the end of her trunk.

Imagine.

It had taken Ed's son Gary a couple of weeks, going to the zoo every day with his father, before the elephants accepted him. But Cupcake liked Mitzi already. After only a few minutes.

Mitzi made a decision. When she grew up, she would be a biologist who specialized in training elephants.

The idea was very comforting. But not so comforting that she forgot her big problem. Two days had gone by, and she was still no closer than she had been on Wednesday to getting her Saint Bernard puppy.

7

Crunch Time at the Zoo

"Old man Harmer had a zoo, EEE-I-EEE-I-O!"
Darwin was singing the new song he had just
made up.

"And in that zoo he had an alligator, EEE-I-
EEE-I-O! With a chomp-chomp here and a
chomp-chomp there, here a chomp, there a
chomp, everywhere a chomp-chomp—"

Mitzi sighed. Darwin was making so much noise
she couldn't talk to Nana Potts. And she had
something very important to discuss.

The three of them were driving to the zoo to
pick up Nana Potts' lunch bucket and shoes,
which Mitzi had forgotten to bring home earlier
in the day.

She had, in fact, forgotten about the lunch
bucket until she came downstairs to dinner.

"Mitzi," hollered Nana Potts. "What did you do with my square-dancing shoes? Miles Hathaway will be here to pick me up at nine o'clock for the Friday Night Barn Dance."

"Oooh," said Mitzi, startled. Partly she was startled about her own forgetfulness. Mostly she was startled by the way Nana Potts looked.

Nana Potts was wearing her frizzy black wig, her dangly purple earrings, her lavender checked square-dancing dress, and a pair of green and white Adidas.

Mitzi did not care for lavender. But in another color (pink) and on someone a little younger (herself), Mitzi would have loved that dress. It had a ruffle on the bottom. And the short skirt, which showed off Nana Potts' bony knees, was so full it stood out straight when she twirled. It also had a lacy white petticoat underneath that was almost as full. Mitzi longed for a pink or blue or even yellow dress exactly like it. But with that frizzy wig, those dangly earrings, and those green Adidas, the dress made Nana Potts look like a sixty-year-old Barbie doll.

And now she was still dressed like that. To take Mitzi to the zoo!

Compared to the way Darwin was dressed, however, Nana Potts looked terrific. Darwin was wearing a pair of summer-weight Big Bird pajamas with a hole in one knee. To hide the hole, he had put on a winter bathrobe that was too small for him. And to hide the fact that he couldn't find its belt, he had tied an old scarf around his waist. He was also wearing his Tyrannosaurus Rex costume. Blue swim fins and Nana Potts' slitty green sunglasses.

Mitzi, who always dressed like a normal person, hoped they would stay in the car. She could find her way alone to Dr. Harmer's office. That was where Ed had told her to pick up the lunch bucket when she had telephoned him after dinner. He also told her that since the zoo was closing soon, Nana Potts could park her car in the employees' lot, just inside the gate.

"And in that zoo he had a gorilla, EEE-I-EEE-I-O! With a harrumph-harrumph here and a harrumph-harrumph there—" sang Darwin.

A snow scraper, which was still in the car from last winter, was bumping her on the head. Mitzi moved it. Then she leaned forward to talk to the back of Nana Potts' wig. "When can you and Mom build a fence for my puppy?"

"Everywhere a harrumph-harrumph—" sang Darwin.

"You'll have to speak up, Mitzi," yelled Nana Potts. "I can't hear you."

Mitzi turned to Darwin. "Why don't you count how many red cars you can see?"

"Chomp-chomp here, chomp-chomp there—" sang Darwin.

Mitzi leaned forward again and spoke louder.

"When can you and Mom build a fence for my puppy?"

"I'm afraid Walter's right, Mitzi. Your mother and I can't do it without help," said Nana Potts.

"Well, can't you talk Walter into helping you?" Mitzi asked.

"Harrumph-harrumph here—" sang Darwin.

"I don't know how. That son of mine is as stubborn as a mule. Gets it from his father, may he rest in peace."

"Here a harrumph, there a harrumph—" sang Darwin.

"Is this the right turn to the zoo?" asked Nana Potts. "I hate driving this time of day. The sun hits me right in the eye."

"NO!" squealed Darwin. "You don't turn right. You turn left." Then he continued his song. "And in that zoo he had a lion, EEE-I-EEE-I-O!"

"With a roar-roar here," joined in Nana Potts. Whooey, thought Mitzi.

Darwin pointed his left index finger. The pinkest one he always sucked. "See, Nana? There's the zoo. I told you to turn left."

"Well, well, so it is. Imagine that," she replied sweetly. "It's a good thing we were along, or Nana would have gotten lost."

In the backseat, Mitzi made a face and edged away from Darwin's car seat. Sometimes Darwin and Nana Potts together were almost more than a normal person could bear.

"Where's the employees' parking lot, Mitzi?"
asked Nana Potts.

Hearing her name, Mitzi sat up straight. She
liked it when people asked her questions they
couldn't answer themselves. "You turn right
there by the gray building," Mitzi told Nana Potts.
Then she took a deep breath and added another
instruction. "You and Darwin stay in the car. I'll
get out and open the gate so you can park. You
don't need to come to Dr. Harmer's office with
me. Darwin can't walk very well in those swim
fins."

Nana Potts thought about that idea as she
pulled the car up to the gate and stopped for Mitzi
to get out. "Well—hurry! It's after eight-thirty
already."

Whew! That was easier than Mitzi had hoped.
Darwin did not suggest taking off his Tyrannosaurus Rex feet and going barefoot. Nana Potts
did not suggest carrying the dinosaur. Normal
Mitzi could walk alone to Dr. Harmer's office
without being embarrassed by crazy-looking rela-
tives singing stupid songs. Even though it was
getting dark, a few visitors remained in the zoo.

Dr. Harmer's office was empty this time of
night. Only one secretary sat at her desk, talking
on the telephone. Realizing what Mitzi had come
for, she pointed to the lunch bucket on a table and
turned her face to the wall to continue her conversation.

No sooner had Mitzi opened the door of the office to go back to the parking lot, than she heard a terrible commotion. First a loud *crunch*. (A car accident?) Then a shrill scream. (Nana Potts?) Then an unending *thump-a-thump-a-thump* as feet pounded toward the employees' parking lot.

Ahead of her, Mitzi saw Ed's familiar figure leave the men's room and streak off in the direction of the trouble.

Mitzi trotted off behind him, but he was too far away to hear her call. Then as she approached the elephant area, something else caught her eye. Pete was hiding in the shadow of the wall around the elephant area. As Ed ran in the opposite direction, Pete softly stole toward the main zoo gate.

Well.

Mitzi trotted toward the parking lot behind Ed, wondering what could have happened. At last, in the graying light, she saw them. Nearly a hundred people formed into a circle in the employees' parking lot. Where had so many people come from? What were they looking at? Fear overtook her. Were Nana Potts and Darwin all right?

Mitzi forgot how weirdly her grandmother and stepbrother were dressed. She forgot the stupid song they had sung. She forgot that she didn't want to be seen with them. She charged off at full speed.

Panting, she pushed her way through the mob.

Oh no!

A tall skinny lady in a short ruffled skirt was standing in the center of the crowd. With one arm, she was protecting a small boy. With the other, she was angrily shaking a snow scraper toward two elephants who had taken over her car. Cupcake had stuck her head partway through the open back door. She was slowly moving her trunk around the inside of the car, searching for something. Daisy was sitting on the dented hood of Nana Potts' blue Rabbit like a queen on her throne.

The snow scraper made wild circles in the air. "You get away from there," Nana Potts yelled. "Do you hear me? Now!"

Ed rushed over and grabbed Nana Potts' arm. "It's okay, lady. I can handle this. You stand back before you get hurt."

Nana Potts backed away, and Ed approached the big elephant cautiously. His voice was loving but firm. "Listen, Daisy, we've had enough nonsense for one day. You know what I mean? Get off that car now, and we'll go back to the elephant house where the comfortable furniture is. Man, we're talking hoses and cool bathwater and brushes and real high-style living. You don't want to sit on a car."

Several gasps escaped from the crowd as Daisy edged off the car and stood on all four feet. Sway-

ing back and forth, she seemed ready to follow Ed
back to the elephant house.

But what about Cupcake? Her trunk was still
moving through the inside of Nana Potts' blue
Rabbit. She was paying no attention to Daisy or
Ed.

Ed looked back and forth between the two elephants. Then he looked at all the people standing
about.

Of course Ed could handle both elephants under normal conditions. But could he do it now?
When he had no elephant hook? When there were
so many people who might do something foolish
and get hurt?

Pete should be here to help him. But Pete had
sneaked off in the other direction. There was only
one person here who might be able to help Ed.

Mitzi. That was who.

Mitzi had watched Ed work with the elephants.
And Cupcake liked Mitzi. Cupcake had stroked
Mitzi on the cheek, the same way she stroked Ed.

Careful to approach Cupcake from the side, not
the back, Mitzi walked toward the car. Then she
spoke to the elephant, trying to make the same
kinds of jokes that Ed would. "Listen, Cupcake.
You won't find any food in that car. I should
know. It belongs to my Nana Potts. Let's go back
to the elephant house where the good stuff is.
We're talking hay and water and maybe even let-
tuce."

More gasps escaped from the crowd as Cupcake backed out of the car and sniffed Mitzi. After Cupcake stroked Mitzi on the cheek, Ed, Mitzi, Daisy, and Cupcake walked slowly toward the elephant house.

Ed kept his eyes on the animals as they walked. He didn't speak to Mitzi until the two big creatures were locked inside their house for the night.

He put his arm around Mitzi and gave her a squeeze. "You're one of us," he said.

Mitzi knew what he meant. Mitzi was one of the people in this world who understood elephants.

Ed wiped his forehead with the back of his hand. "Man, that was sweaty. I guess I should be glad it didn't turn out worse. But I'll give it to you straight. I really wanted to be an elephant keeper. And it hurts like anything to have the shortest career in history. Would you believe we're talking exactly one day?"

"What do you mean one day?" Mitzi demanded. "You're not going to quit, are you?"

"No way, man. I'm going to get fired. Locking up properly is an absolute rule here," Ed explained. "Especially with dangerous animals like elephants. And I know I did it. I remember checking the lock on the house and the lock on the gate just before I went to the men's room to wash up before going home. Someone must have come by after me and unlocked those doors."

"Pete," said Mitzi.

Ed shrugged. "I wouldn't put it past him. But there's no way I could ever prove it."

"Well, I can prove it," said Mitzi. "I saw him."

"You saw him unlock the doors?" Ed asked.

"Well—no," said Mitzi. "But I saw him in the elephant area when everyone else was running to the parking lot. He sure looked guilty about something."

Ed sighed. "That doesn't exactly prove he did it. Harmer wouldn't believe me if I told him that, anyway. Charlie is Pete's uncle, remember. And Charlie has been at the zoo longer than anybody. Even Harmer."

"Well, maybe Dr. Harmer will believe me. I'll ask my stepfather to take me to his house tonight so I can tell him what happened," Mitzi said. "Before he finds out about it from anyone else."

The wrinkles almost disappeared from Ed's forehead. "Yeah. It really might help if you could talk to him first. Are you sure your stepfather will take you tonight?"

"Yes," said Mitzi, as if she really believed it. But would Walter take her? When he was too busy to build a fence for her puppy or do anything except work on his book?

When she got back to the parking lot, it was almost dark. Nana Potts was strapping Darwin into his car seat.

She turned and patted Mitzi on the head. "Well, I guess we showed all those people how to handle an elephant. I'm just sorry that stubborn son of mine wasn't here to see it. Maybe he'd realize that people who can handle elephants deserve to own a puppy."

Mitzi set down the lunch bucket she was still carrying. "Nana Potts, can't you help me think of something? I've got to make Walter change his mind about building that fence. I only have two and a half weeks."

Nana Potts waved her hand in the air. "Two and a half weeks is longer than I have to solve my problems. I've got to figure out how to make my insurance company pay to have my car repaired. But before that, I've got to figure out how to get home when I can't see."

"You can't see?" Mitzi asked, frightened.

"Not a thing," said Nana Potts. "That fool elephant broke the headlights on my car. We'll have to sit in front with Nana, Mitzi. We'll have to be Nana's extra pair of eyes."

Yes, Nana Potts did need an extra pair of eyes in front. Even though she gripped the wheel tightly with both hands and leaned forward to study the road through her thick glasses, she had a hard time steering. She kept weaving back and forth between lanes. She nearly bumped into a truck parked at the curb. And she scared two delivery boys crossing the street so badly that they yelled and scattered bagels in the air like snowflakes.

So it was hard work for Mitzi to keep calm. She not only had to watch the road, but she had to think about how to persuade Walter to build a fence while listening to the terrible racket coming from the backseat. Louder than ever, Darwin was singing the new verse he had made up to his song.

Old man Harmer had a zoo,
    EEE-I-EEE-I-O!
And in that zoo he had two elephants,
    EEE-I-EEE-I-O!
With a crunch-crunch here
    and a crunch-crunch there,
Here a crunch, there a crunch,
    everywhere a crunch-crunch.
Old man Harmer had a zoo,
    EEE-I-EEE-I-O!

8

Good News and Bad News

As Mitzi told the story about Nana Potts' car and the elephants, Dr. Harmer sat silent. Now and then, he closed his eyes. Or tapped the ends of his ten fingers together, making a round cage. Or dropped his head down so Mitzi could see the long strands of hair he combed from one side over the top to cover his bald spot. But he said nothing.

Mitzi couldn't stand it. "Well, what are you going to do to Pete?"

"I don't know yet," Dr. Harmer replied. "I'll have to hear his side of the story first."

Hmmph. Mitzi sure wouldn't have to hear Pete's side of the story first. She sure would know what to do. She kicked the leg of Dr. Harmer's desk, waiting for a better answer.

Walter stood up first. "Well, we better be going, Mitzi. It's past your bedtime. And I still want to work on my manuscript tonight."

Dr. Harmer stood up next, holding out his hand. "Thanks for coming, Walter. I know how busy you are."

Mitzi stood up last. Wasn't anyone going to thank *her*? She was the one who had seen Pete in the elephant area. She was the one who had persuaded Walter to come to Dr. Harmer's house. She was the one who had reported the whole story. No. No one was going to thank her. Walter and Dr. Harmer were walking out the door of the study, talking about boring things like contracts and deadlines. Mitzi sighed and followed them.

Well, at least Ed would call and thank her first thing Saturday morning.

But Ed didn't call first thing in the morning. Mitzi scowled as she crossed off the *13* on her calendar. It was only fair for Ed to let her know things were all right at the zoo so she could start worrying about her own problems again. She didn't have much time left.

The hours dragged on, and still the phone didn't ring. By Saturday night, Mitzi feared the worst. Ed didn't call because he had been fired. She hadn't saved his job at all.

On Sunday, she crossed off the *14* on her calendar. Then she started looking for Ed's number in the phone book. There was no Ed Porter listed.

Worry made her cranky. She told Darwin to stop singing his stupid zoo song. She told Frederick to stop scratching his stupid arm. She told Nana Potts that she hated baked beans with green peppers and bacon, even though she had loved baked beans with green peppers and bacon just last month.

Then Sunday night, as she was brushing her teeth before going to bed, the phone rang. Ed was calling Mitzi with so much news she could hardly keep track of it all. Some of it was good news. And some of it was bad news.

Bad News: Dr. Harmer never even asked Pete about what Mitzi saw.

Good News: Because Pete and Charlie had both quit.

Bad News: They left because they got better jobs from another relative, in the construction business.

Good News: Ed had been promoted to Charlie's job as the main elephant keeper.

Bad News: The zoo was now understaffed. Ed had to work in both the zebra and giraffe area and the elephant area until Dr. Harmer could replace Pete and Charlie.

Good News: Ed took his son Gary to the zoo with him on Sunday, and Gary was a big help.

Bad News: Gary had a terrible attack of asthma when they got home, and the doctor said he couldn't go back to the zoo Monday.

Good News: Geronimo, the zoo's baby giraffe, would be one year old tomorrow. Newspaper reporters and TV crews would be coming at twelve o'clock to take pictures of him with his birthday cake.

Bad News: Ed's son Gary, who had been asked to present the cake to Geronimo on television, would not be able to do it.

Good News: Both Dr. Harmer and Ed thought Mitzi would be a wonderful substitute for Gary on television.

Bad News: Dr. Harmer had ordered a very large birthday cake, and Mitzi couldn't lift it alone.

Best News of All: Ed and Dr. Harmer wanted Mitzi to invite another child to help her present the cake to Geronimo the giraffe. Ed didn't want her to invite Darwin because he wasn't strong enough to lift the cake. Dr. Harmer didn't want her to invite Darwin because he was worried about what Darwin might say on television.

Smiling, Mitzi hung up and told her family the wonderful news about her television appearance tomorrow. Would Frederick like to go to the zoo and help her give the cake to Geronimo?

No. Frederick would not. Frederick, who had an accordion lesson at eleven o'clock, did not care to cancel it to go to a birthday party for a giraffe.

So Mitzi telephoned Elsie Wolf.

Elsie not only *did* want to go to Geronimo's party, but she was as excited about being on television as Mitzi was.

Together they made a list of all the people they could think of. Tomorrow they would call everyone and tell them to watch television at noon.

Mitzi went to bed, planning what she would wear. This time her television appearance would be perfect. This time Darwin would not be along.

9

Geronimo's
One-derful Birthday Party

Mitzi crossed off the *15* on her calendar. She was so excited about being on television that she didn't have time to worry about her puppy's fence this morning. She still had sixteen days left to worry about that.

As they drove in the car to pick up Elsie Wolf, Mitzi looked at her mother. "I like it when we do things together. Just the two of us."

Her mother took one hand off the steering wheel and squeezed Mitzi's knee. "I like it too, honey."

Mitzi studied her mother's profile. The mouth that turned up pleasantly at the corners. The straight, ladylike nose. The shiny brown hair, lightly fluffed. Mitzi hoped she would look just like her mother when she grew up.

"You don't feel bad that I didn't invite you, do you?" Mitzi asked.

"Invite me to do what?" her mother asked.

"To be on television with me," said Mitzi. "To help me give the birthday cake to Geronimo."

Her mother smiled. "I think that Elsie was the perfect person for you to invite. You and Elsie are two of the prettiest little girls I know. Almost like twins. You'll look very nice together on TV."

Mitzi smoothed the pleats on her new green-and-brown plaid skirt. She did feel very grown-up-looking today. Her light brown hair was freshly washed with new green ribbons above each ear. Although she would have chosen another blouse if she'd had the chance (Dr. Harmer had called and asked her to wear Frederick's SUPPORT YOUR LOCAL ZOO T-shirt), she did like the way the green T-shirt and her plaid skirt matched. She wiggled her toes happily inside her brown oxfords.

When they turned into the driveway of the Wolfs' house, Elsie and her mother were waiting on the porch. Her mother gave Elsie a kiss and waved good-bye. Then Elsie walked prettily down the steps.

There she was, flashing her big dimples. Her lacy pink dress was covered with a ruffled pinafore of eyelet embroidery. Her flaxen-colored hair hung softly past her shoulders. Her black Mary

Jane shoes were so shiny you could see your face in them.

Elsie and Mitzi did not look like twins. They looked like Alice in Wonderland and the Mock Turtle.

Elsie was too polite to mention Frederick's T-shirt. All she said was, "I like your pleated skirt, Mitzi. I'll get in back so I won't crowd you and get it wrinkled." She settled herself in the middle of the backseat, carefully spreading lace and ruffles in all directions.

Mitzi tucked the green T-shirt more tightly into her waistband. "That's a pretty dress, Elsie. Is it new?"

"Thank you," said Elsie politely. "Mama thought I should have a new outfit since I'm going to be on television for the first time. And it *is* a birthday party." Her eyes avoided Mitzi's outfit.

Suddenly Mitzi remembered how she had fallen down the first time she had worn her plaid skirt. Suddenly she remembered why Nana Potts had washed it. Trying not to remember, she changed the subject. "Did you make your phone calls?" she asked Elsie.

"No," Elsie said. "It took so much time to find this dress that I didn't have time. But Mama gave the list to Daddy's secretary and told her to call everyone. Mr. Ledgard, too."

"Oh," said Mitzi, disappointed. Mr. Ledgard was the janitor at Amelia Earhart Elementary, the most important person in their school. Elsie shouldn't have a secretary call him. She should do it herself.

Unable to think of anything else to say, Mitzi turned forward and looked out the window. But Elsie kept up a long conversation with Mitzi's mother. She wanted to thank her for driving them to the zoo. Her own mother couldn't bear missing the chance to watch Elsie on television.

When they reached the giraffe area, a huge crowd was milling about. Boys wearing jeans. Girls wearing shorts. Parents wearing tired looks on their faces. Elsie seemed very overdressed in her Alice in Wonderland costume, and Mitzi began to feel a little better.

Inside the fence, about a dozen cakes were set on the grass in a half circle. White cakes. Chocolate cakes. Cakes with rosebuds and candles. Newspaper cameramen were squatting on the ground, studying the cakes from different sides. TV cameramen were walking about, carrying huge cameras on their shoulders. Newscasters were checking their mikes. Babies in the crowd were crying.

Dr. Harmer spotted Mitzi and rushed over. "There you are!" he cried, sounding breathless. A breeze had blown the long hairs from the top of his head. They were hanging over one ear.

He took Mitzi and Elsie inside the gate and showed them the special cake that he had ordered. The big one that Mitzi and Elsie would carry. Nearly three feet long, it was covered with yellow frosting. On the top was a frosting giraffe with brown spots. And in brown letters the cake said *Geronimo Is One-derful.*

"Ooh," cooed Elsie. "Isn't that darling."

Hmmph, thought Mitzi. The cake wasn't darling at all. The person who made it couldn't even spell *wonderful.*

Then Dr. Harmer showed Mitzi and Elsie how to lift the cake and where to stand. The cameras would shift to them as soon as Ed led the giraffe out the door of his house.

Before Mitzi realized what was happening, the cameras were grinding. Mikes were shoved in Dr. Harmer's face, and he was telling the people of Kansas what fun everyone was having today at the zoo. "Keep your nickels and dimes coming, boys and girls. And tell your parents to mail their dollars. The zoo needs lots of money to care for these wonderful animals we have here."

No one had told Dr. Harmer to comb his hair. The long strands were still hanging over one ear.

Then Ed led Geronimo out of the giraffe house by a rope. Someone had put a cardboard party hat on his head and hung paper streamers around his long neck.

"Now," whispered Elsie, reaching for her end of the cake. Mitzi reached for her end, too, and the girls held the cake as high as they could. It was

heavy and awkward, and Mitzi wondered how long they were supposed to hold it. Maybe Geronimo would walk over and take a bite.

But Geronimo did not like his cake. He did not like the crowd of boys and girls who were whistling and stamping. He strained at his rope, trying to run.

All at once, Mitzi did not like the party, either. It was not right to put a hat on a giraffe. It was not right to whistle at him and scare him like that. She was sorry she had come.

But it was too late. A dozen cameras were pointed at the girls. When someone waved and motioned for them to smile, Elsie showed her dimples. Mitzi tried hard not to scowl.

Then suddenly the program was over, and reporters packed up their cameras to leave. As Ed turned to lead Geronimo back inside the giraffe house, a boy cried out, "What about the cake? You didn't give him any cake!"

"Geronimo doesn't eat cake," Ed called back over his shoulder.

Shouts of protest rose from the crowd.

Looking flushed from the heat, Dr. Harmer reached for his loose strands of hair and wound them over his bald spot. He cleared his throat, getting ready to speak.

"How would you boys and girls like to eat Geronimo's birthday cakes?" he asked loudly.

Instantly the protests turned to shouts of pleasure. Dr. Harmer smiled graciously, unlocked the gate, and waited for the children to enter.

He didn't wait long. Hands pushed. Elbows poked. Feet kicked. Children poured into the giraffe area like marbles from a bag.

"Slow down, children," cried Dr. Harmer, ducking to one side. "Stop running. Show us your manners."

Any manners the children once might have had were left outside the gate. As soon as they realized there were no knives with which to cut the cakes, they dived in with their fists—sometimes both hands at once. Now and then, a child tried to lick the sweet stuff from a messy hand. But soon they realized it was more fun to throw the cake than to eat it. Through the air hunks sailed, soared, flittered, and fell.

My goodness! thought Mitzi as a wad of orange sponge cake hit her borrowed T-shirt.

"You cut that out!" she howled as a glob of chocolate frosting splattered on her new plaid skirt.

Hearing the commotion, Ed rushed from the giraffe house to help Dr. Harmer. Together they shooed the gooey children back through the gate, and peace was restored.

Outside the gate, parents were scolding their grimy children.

Inside the gate, no one spoke.

The grass was pimpled with colored hunks. Yellow cake. Orange cake. Pink cake. Chocolate cake. White cake. Spice cake.

Elsie looked at the mess through slitty eyes. Her dimples had disappeared.

Mitzi picked up a paper plate that had held one of the cakes and tried to scrape the chocolate frosting off her skirt.

Ed licked the end of his moustache, looking hopeless.

Dr. Harmer looked at his watch.

"What a mess," called Mitzi's mother across the fence. "Can I help you clean it up?"

Dr. Harmer arranged his face into a smile. "Of course not, Patricia. You'll get dirty. No, Ed can clean this place up."

Mitzi was stunned. Who said Ed could clean this place up? He didn't make the mess. He was in the giraffe house when it happened. The person who had let the kids in the gate and told them to eat the cake when there weren't any knives was Dr. Harmer, that's who.

"No, Ed can't clean it up," Mitzi howled. "He doesn't have time."

"Mitzi—" her mother scolded gently.

"Well, it's true," Mitzi fumed. "He's already doing the work of three people because this zoo doesn't have enough keepers."

"Well, what do you expect us to do about it?" Elsie demanded. "I can't clean that yuck up. I have on my very best dress that Mama just bought me this morning."

Mitzi bit her lip. Then suddenly an idea hit her. A terrific idea. "I know!" she exclaimed. "We can bring Cupcake over and let her eat these crumbs. She flips over cake."

Ed smiled his colored-lights smile and clapped Mitzi on the shoulder. "Man, why didn't I think of that! Would you believe we've got a real elephant lady here?"

After Ed and Mitzi led Cupcake to the giraffe area, she had a wonderful time. She poked her trunk through the grass, flicking all kinds of goodies into her mouth. When the cake had disappeared and the grass looked green again, Cupcake knew exactly whom to thank for her invitation to the birthday party. She stroked Mitzi with the tip of her trunk, leaving the last few crumbs of cake and frosting on Mitzi's face and hair.

"You need a bath," Elsie told her.

Mitzi didn't mind being dirty. It felt great to be petted by an elephant.

As they walked to the gate, Mitzi's mother put her arm around her daughter. "Ed's right. You have a special way with animals. Just like Walter. I wish he could have been here to see you."

For a minute, Mitzi was tempted to tell her mother that she was better with animals than Walter was. If Walter liked animals, he would hurry and build a fence so Mitzi could have a puppy.

But this was not the time to discuss fences. Not when Elsie Wolf was along. Mitzi had not yet told Elsie there was trouble about the fence and that she might not be able to accept the puppy.

Somehow it wasn't fair. Elsie didn't love animals the way Mitzi did, but she was going to get a puppy anyway.

How come life was always so easy for Elsie? She never had to worry about anything. Mitzi sighed as she looked at her friend. Elsie was probably the only child inside the giraffe area today who had managed to stay clean. In her white and pink Alice in Wonderland costume, she still looked as fresh and sparkly as sugar on a gumdrop.

10

The "Who Am I?" Game

"No, Mitzi. I don't have time to build a fence before the end of the month. And I don't want you to ask me again." Walter tightened his strong, square fingers around the steering wheel. He looked grim.

Mitzi slunk down in the front seat, away from him. Stepfathers should love their little girls. But Walter didn't love Mitzi any more than the ugly old stepmother loved Cinderella. And he was just as mean.

Elsie Wolf, who lived with both her *real* parents, was loved. Elsie Wolf's father had nearly finished the fence he was building for their backyard. Elsie Wolf would be bringing her puppy home in six days, right on schedule.

But only a miracle could save Mitzi's puppy.

85

Today was August 25. Mitzi had less than a week to pick up her puppy, or Elsie's uncle would sell it.

Mitzi screwed up her face, longing to cry. Maybe she would feel better if she could cry.

Only this morning she had gone with Elsie to see the puppies again. Only this morning she had felt like the happiest girl in the world, watching the adorable puppies that had grown faster than bean sprouts since she had last seen them. Seven wiggly bundles of fur that seemed all ears and paws. How warm she had felt holding her soon-to-be-very-own puppy in her arms. And Elsie was right. The gray ones were better. Gray fur made them look more like elephants.

But now her hopes of owning that puppy were gone. What right did Walter have to go to the zoo to talk to Dr. Harmer again when he didn't have time to build a fence?

"Old man Harmer had a zoo, EEE-I-EEE-I-O!" sang Darwin from the backseat.

"Can the concert, will you?" complained Frederick, who was sitting next to him. "We've been listening to that song for two weeks."

"And in that zoo he had a penguin, EEE-I-EEE-I-O! With a waddle-waddle here and a waddle-waddle there, here a waddle—" sang Darwin.

"Let's play a game," suggested Frederick. "Didn't they teach you any games in that preschool Nana took you to yesterday?"

"*Yeah!*" said Darwin. "Let's play 'Who Am I?' I get to be first. Okay, who am I?"

"Hmmm," said Frederick, pretending to be thinking. "That's a hard one. Uh— You're a tryannosaurus rex with a brontosaurus bone in your mouth."

"Wrong!" squealed Darwin. "Guess again."

"Well, then you're a brontosaurus with a tyrannosaurus rex bone in your mouth," guessed Frederick.

"DUMMY!" hollered Darwin. "Brontosauruses don't eat tyrannosaurus rexes. Your turn to guess, Mitzi."

Mitzi did not care to guess. She did not even care to turn around to see what Darwin was doing. "No," she grumbled.

"You better play, Mitzi," Frederick urged. "Or Pavarotti is going to screech our ears off."

Mitzi did not know who Pavarotti was. But she certainly knew who was likely to screech their ears off. She turned around and looked at Darwin.

Sitting in his little car seat, the dumb genius was folding his hands together and holding his arms out straight. Anyone knew that's what kindergarten babies and preschoolers did when they were pretending to be an elephant.

"You're an el—" she started to say. But then she saw Frederick winking at her. Frederick wanted her to go on making wrong guesses so Darwin wouldn't sing his stupid song.

87

Quickly Mitzi corrected herself. "You're an alligator," she guessed.

"Wrong!" crowed Darwin. "Frederick's turn. I'll give you a hint. I'm gray."

"Let's see," said Frederick, scratching his head. "Are you a steam shovel?"

Darwin shrieked with delight. "No, no, no! I'll give you more hints, Mitzi. I have wrinkled skin. And a big long nose. And I'm mean to people I don't like."

"You're Walter," Mitzi said without thinking.

In the front seat next to Mitzi, Walter let out a hoot. "Is that an opinion about my looks or my character?"

At least he was smiling. Sort of. Maybe now was a good time to tell him. Maybe now she should say, "If you loved me, like a real father, you'd build me a fence so I could have the puppy Elsie's uncle promised me."

But before she could speak, he reached out a hairy arm and put it around her shoulder. "Mitzi, Patricia and Mother have both told me how good you are with animals. And all of us want you to have a dog. We really do. Maybe when my textbook is finished in a few weeks, I can start building a fence. I'm sure I'll have it finished in time to get you a puppy for Christmas."

Christmas!

Christmas was one of those things too far away

even to think about—like wearing high-heeled shoes or driving a car.

Walter removed his arm from Mitzi's shoulder, pulled the car into the parking lot, and started barking orders. "Frederick, help Darwin out of his car seat. And be sure to keep an eye on him when you go to the alligator house. Mitzi, don't forget your cake."

With a sigh, Mitzi picked up the carrot and zucchini cake with whole wheat flour that Nana Potts had baked for Cupcake. The cake part had been Mitzi's idea. When she heard she was coming to the zoo, she asked Nana Potts to bake something special for Cupcake. But the carrots and zucchini and whole wheat had been Nana Potts' idea. "If that fool elephant is going to eat dessert all day long, she better eat some with vitamins in," Nana Potts had said.

The whole point of the present was so that Mitzi would have something special along to teach Cupcake to kneel. If Mitzi could teach an elephant to do a trick, maybe Walter would realize Mitzi was big enough to train a Saint Bernard.

But that idea wouldn't work now. Nothing would work now.

Darwin trotted toward the gate with Frederick behind. And Walter headed toward Dr. Harmer's office, whistling merrily.

No one even cared that this was the very worst day of Mitzi's whole life.

11

A Cake for Cupcake
and a Cupcake for Mitzi

When Mitzi reached the elephant area, a man she had never seen before was shoveling something into plastic bags. Ed and the elephants were nowhere in sight.

"Who are *you?*" Mitzi asked, realizing too late that the question wasn't polite. She hated it when people dialed the wrong phone number and then asked *her* that dumb question.

The man, who was probably the new elephant keeper, seemed too busy to answer. *Scrape* went his shovel. *Scrape.* Standing on her tiptoes, Mitzi looked over the wall to see what was so much more interesting than she was.

Manure, that's what. The man was shoveling elephant manure.

"Where are Cupcake and Daisy?" Mitzi asked.

"In the elephant house." *Scrape.*

If the elephants were in their house, how come the gate to the area was locked? During zoo hours, the elephants should be outside, or people should be allowed inside the building. "Well, let me in," Mitzi ordered. "I want to see them."

The man shook his head. "No visitors in the elephant house today."

Hmmph, thought Mitzi. How dare that man treat her like a plain old zoo visitor. She was Mitzi McAllister, friend of Cupcake and Daisy and future biologist and elephant trainer. "How come?" she demanded.

"Orders," said the man.

Mitzi scowled at that unsatisfactory answer. "I want to see Ed."

"Ed's in the elephant house. And he said not to let any visitors in there today. Go see the monkeys. Or the penguins," suggested the man.

A breeze brought the smell of manure to Mitzi's nose. Yuck. "I didn't come here to see any monkeys or penguins. I came to bring a cake to Cupcake. You tell Ed that Mitzi is here with a carrot and zucchini whole wheat cake for Cupcake."

So there, she thought, feeling very brave.

The man shrugged, as if he didn't care too much one way or the other. "Okay." He laid down his shovel.

In a minute, he was back from the elephant house. "Ed says you can come in."

Once the man had led Mitzi through the door

into the dark and silent elephant house, she felt less brave. How come there wasn't any light in here? How come the elephants weren't sloshing in their water trough or making their friendly trumpeting sounds?

Everything was so strange and silent that Mitzi was sorry she had asked the man to bring her. Worst of all, her eyes were still so dazzled from the sunshine outdoors that she couldn't see.

She almost turned and left. But Ed called out in a hoarse voice. "Bring her into the stall, Marvin. She'll be okay."

Mitzi knew about the stall. It was the part of the building where the elephants stayed. The part that was separated from the visitors by a thick wall. Keepers went inside the stall, but never any visitors. To get to it, you had to go through the keepers' room.

As Marvin led Mitzi into the keepers' room, he took the cake from her and put it on a shelf. After leading her through a third door into the elephant stall, Marvin disappeared.

Mitzi widened her eyes to make out the strange shadows in the stall. In one corner, a big gray thing was spread out on the floor. Was it Cupcake? Yes, of course. She was lying on her side with her eyes closed. Ed was stretched next to her on a cot, one arm resting on Cupcake's big neck. Daisy stood alone, looking pitiful.

Ed sat up on his cot and rubbed his chin. "I'm

glad you've come, Mitzi. Man, I could use your help." His voice sounded raspy.

"But I thought that man—Marvin—was your new helper," Mitzi said.

"Yeah. Harmer hired him last week. And he's okay on the business end of a shovel, if you know what I mean," said Ed. "But elephants make him nervous. And sick elephants turn him to Jell-O."

Mitzi bit her lip. "Is Cupcake sick?" she asked.

"Pneumonia," said Ed. "Man, I haven't had any sleep for two days." He looked like it, too. Mitzi could see his eyes now, and they were an icky red color. "I've been here all this time," Ed went on. "The vet told me to feed her peanut butter with penicillin every two hours and to coax her to stand up."

"She shouldn't stand up if she's sick," Mitzi informed him. "My mother always makes me go to bed when I'm sick."

"Listen, that's a good idea for people but a bad idea for elephants. Elephants can sleep standing up. But if they lie down when they're sick, sometimes they—" Ed cleared his froggy throat and started over. "Sometimes they never stand up again. I mean, who could lift them? Not you or me, man."

What was Ed trying to say? Was Cupcake going to die?

Suddenly Mitzi threw her arms around Ed's

waist, clinging desperately as her body shook. All those problems she had thought she had didn't matter anymore. All those fake tears she had tried to cry seemed stupid and selfish. She was crying real tears now.

Ed was crying, too. Mitzi could feel his wet cheeks against her forehead.

At last, Mitzi pulled away and wiped her eyes with the back of her hand. "What do you want me to do?"

"You don't mind helping, do you?" said Ed. "Listen, I can't think of anyone else to ask. The doctor says Gary is allergic to hay and won't let him come here anymore."

Of course Mitzi didn't mind. "What do you want me to do?" she said louder.

"Sit on that cot and talk to Cupcake. I mean *talk* to her. Let her know you love her. Let her know you want her to get well. Let her know you don't want her to fall asleep lying down. Scratch her behind the ears. She loves that. And if you're not afraid to stick your hand in her mouth—she won't bite you—you can rub her tongue. Having her tongue rubbed is her favorite sport in the world," Ed instructed.

"What are you going to do?" Mitzi asked. "Try to take a nap?"

"No way. I don't have time for fun and games. I've got to take care of Daisy," said Ed.

"Is Daisy sick, too?" Mitzi asked.

"If she isn't now, she soon will be." Ed stood up. "Look at her. She knows what it means when a sick elephant lies down. Man, I swear she's been crying for two days. She feels like a mother to Cupcake, even though that little girl acts like a spoiled brat sometimes. Daisy hasn't touched her food since Cupcake has been sick. I'm afraid I'll have two dead elephants on my hands if I can't coax her to eat. Will you help me?" Ed begged.

For answer, Mitzi sat down on the cot and started talking to Cupcake. "Listen, Cupcake, I love you, and I'm going to see that you get well. So don't you dare fall asleep lying down because I won't let you. I'm going to scratch you behind the ears and tickle you to keep you awake if I have to. So there."

Cupcake recognized her friend. She raised her trunk limply off the floor and waved it at Mitzi.

"Good girl, Cupcake! Good girl!" Mitzi cried. "Just for that, I'm going to rub your tongue."

She slid off the cot and sat on the cool floor at Cupcake's side. Bravely Mitzi stuck her hand in the elephant's mouth and rubbed Cupcake's tongue. Cupcake opened her eyes and looked gratefully at Mitzi.

Mitzi knew she should keep talking to the ele-

phant. But she had run out of things to say. It was easier to sing a song. She started loudly with the only song she could think of.

> Old man Harmer had a zoo,
>   EEE-I-EEE-I-O!
> And in that zoo he had a Cupcake,
>   EEE-I-EEE-I-O!
> With a rub-rub here
>   and a rub-rub there,
> Here a rub, there a rub,
>   everywhere a rub-rub.
> Old man Harmer had a zoo
>   EEE-I-EEE-I-O!

From across the stall, Ed joined in.

> And in that zoo he had a Daisy,
>   EEE-I-EEE-I-O!
> With some hay-hay here
>   and some hay-hay there,
> Here some hay, there some hay,
>   everywhere some hay-hay—

The music cheered everyone. Daisy began to eat the hay. Ed began to sound like a person instead of a worn-out engine. Cupcake began to wave her trunk weakly back and forth. And Mitzi began to get an idea.

A terrific idea!

She ran over to Ed. "I know how we can do it," she cried. "I know how we can stand Cupcake up."

"Listen, Mitzi," said Ed. "Cupcake is no bantamweight. We're talking two or three tons."

"We're not going to lift her. Daisy is," Mitzi explained. "Daisy can do it. She's lots bigger than Cupcake. And you said Daisy understands Cupcake has to get up."

Ed licked his moustache. "I don't think it will work, Mitzi. Daisy could help Cupcake if Cupcake would put out a little effort herself. But Daisy can't do it alone."

"Well, I'll make Cupcake try. I'll show her the cake Nana Potts baked for her and make her try. You make Daisy help her," Mitzi said.

Ed took a deep breath. "Well, we sure don't have anything to lose, man."

Mitzi ran into the keepers' room and got Nana Potts' cake from the shelf. Ed brought Daisy over next to Cupcake and showed her how to lift Cupcake with her trunk.

"Listen, Daisy," said Ed. "I'll give it to you straight. You pull this job off right, and I'll give you an extra head of cabbage every day."

"See this cake, Cupcake?" said Mitzi. "You stand up on all four feet, and I'll let you eat the whole thing."

Daisy strained. Cupcake whimpered. And slowly, slowly Cupcake rose to her feet.

"We did it!" screamed Mitzi as she jumped into the air.

"We did it!" screamed Mitzi as she twirled with happiness.

"We did it!" screamed Mitzi as she bumped headlong into Walter, who had come into the elephant stall with Dr. Harmer and Mitzi's brothers.

"You sure did," Walter said, giving her a squeeze. "I'm really proud of you."

Mitzi pulled away, feeling mixed up. Part of her was very happy. But part of her was ashamed. Looking down, she kicked the toe of one shoe with the other. "I'm sorry I pestered you so much about the fence. I know I made you mad."

"And I'm sorry I made you mad," said Walter. "I am pretty stubborn sometimes. I get it from my mother."

Mitzi smiled. That wasn't *exactly* what Nana Potts had said.

"I just realized something, Mitzi," said Walter. "It's not written anywhere that *I* have to do all the repairs around the house just because I like to. I think we should hire someone to build a fence so you can get that Saint Bernard next week."

Mitzi caught her breath. Did he really mean it? Then suddenly she threw her arms around him. "Oh, Daddy!"

"There's just one thing," said Walter. "Even if the puppy has gray hair and wrinkled skin and a long, ugly nose, I don't want you to name him Walter."

Mitzi laughed. "I can't. It's a girl puppy. And I'm going to name her Cupcake."

Everything You Need to Know About

SPORTS INJURIES

Professional athletes condition their bodies to avoid sports injuries.

Everything You Need to Know About
SPORTS INJURIES

Lawrence Clayton, Ph.D.

THE ROSEN PUBLISHING GROUP, INC.
NEW YORK

Published in 1995, 1999 by The Rosen Publishing Group, Inc.
29 East 21st Street, New York, NY 10010

Revised Edition 1999

Library of Congress Cataloging-in-Publication Data

Clayton, L. (Lawrence)
    Everything you need to know about sports injuries / Lawrence Clayton.
       p. cm. — (The Need to know library)
    Includes bibliographical references and index.
    ISBN 0-8239-2875-6
    1. Sports injuries—Juvenile literature. [1. Sports injuries.] I. Title. II. Series.
RD97.C583 1995
617.1'027—dc20
                                              94-26983
                                               CIP
                                              AC

Manufactured in the United States of America

Contents

Nearly everyone suffers some sort of physical injury from playing
sports.

Chapter 1

How Dangerous Is Your Sport?

Remember the first day you went out for football—or track or baseball, swimming or tennis? There was one thing on your mind, and it wasn't getting injured. You probably were thinking, "This is going to be fun!" You were going to be part of the action.

You've probably had your share of cuts and bruises, scrapes and broken bones just cruising around the neighborhood or skateboarding or playing basketball or football with your friends. Your parents may have taught you safety rules. But now you are older, your body is larger, and your muscle strength is greater. You may not realize that when size and speed increase, the chances of injury also increase.

Now you may be participating in organized sports. If so, you should be pushing yourself to meet greater challenges, and your coach should be showing you the difference between just "knocking around" with your friends and being a trained athlete.

Most of the time participation in organized sports is less risky than just playing around; your school should have the resources to deal with injuries. But the motivation and intensity that you devote to becoming an accomplished athlete should also include conditioning your body and preparing your mind to meet the challenges and deal with risks.

Growth of Sports

In 1991, it was estimated that about 50 percent of boys and 25 percent of girls between the ages of 8 and 16 competed in an organized sports program sometime during the year. People used to think that competitive sports were more suited to boys than to girls, but that view is changing; between 1976 and 1991, female involvement in high school sports is estimated to have increased by 700 percent.

As sports have become increasingly popular with both male and female adolescents, they have also become their second most frequent cause of injury. The National Youth Sports Safety Foundation estimated that more than 5 million children visit hospital emergency rooms each year for treatment of sports injuries—and most of those injuries were from unorganized activities or simple play.

While about 95 percent of sports injuries are minor—bruises, muscle pulls, sprains, strains, and cuts or abrasions—it is estimated that 7 to 10 percent of all spinal injuries occur during sports, especially diving, surfing, and football. Such injuries can range from a neck sprain or pinched nerve to more serious conditions, including paralysis or death.

Growth of Injuries

Any injury can be serious, so how do we explain why so many injuries happen in the first place? Is it because more young men and women participate in sports every year? Or is it because injury prevention is not stressed as part of their program of sports training?

Comparing the increasing numbers of athletes with the number of injuries can be oversimplifying. That is not the only thing to consider. We can ask why 60 percent of all football injuries happen before the first game of the season, while the players are learning to adapt to the demands of the sport. Wouldn't greater concentration on injury prevention, conditioning, and off-season training drastically reduce this statistic? (Chapter 8 discusses this in greater detail.)

No one wants to be one of the thousands of young people who end up frustrated and depressed because of sports injuries. So why do we take the attitude that pain can be tolerated and ignored when common sense tells us that our bodies can take only so much abuse? This attitude contributes to injuries. A lifetime of enjoying your favorite sports can be sacrificed

because "the game" is often considered more important than the players.

Seeking Help

Concentration on learning how your body works
and how to make it work well can make all the difference. When everyone is saying largely, "No pain, no
gain," it takes courage to admit that you're hurting
and need help. Remember, nothing is as important as
your health.

Many factors must be dealt with when you compete
in any sport: your own ambition to excel, awareness
of what your parents and your friends think of you,
steps to condition your body, and the right attitude.
It's a big job. It takes a mature person to do it.

Don't get the idea, however, that all sports injuries
happen at school. Each year about 300,000 children
under 16 are treated in emergency rooms for bike-
related injuries. One in three of those injuries is to the
head, and 85 percent of bike-related deaths are from
head injuries. These statistics prove the importance of
always wearing a helmet when biking. In some places,
helmets are even required by law: Pennsylvania enact-
ed a state law in 1995 requiring all bicyclists under 12
to wear helmets, with fines for the parents of those
who don't obey.

If you follow your doctor's orders, it shouldn't be
long before you're back to your regular routine. It may
seem twice as hard to wait while you recuperate from

Sometimes people try to push their bodies too hard. That's when injuries occur.

some "dumb" accident, but blaming yourself—or anyone else—won't make it any easier.

In the meantime, remember one thing on which the experts agree: You are special. There is no one exactly like you, with your abilities. So don't compare your recovery—or your injuries—with anyone else's. You will recover at your own rate, just as you do everything else.

Chapter 2

Head Injuries

Injuries to the head range from simple bruises and cuts to fractures and brain injuries, including concussion (a violent jolt to the brain). A bruise may cause tenderness, swelling, and discoloration of the skin because the blood vessels under the skin rupture and bleed into underlying tissue. A minor bump on the head should be treated with an ice pack. A bag of frozen vegetables or a plastic bag filled with ice cubes works well; cover it with a towel and apply to the injured spot.

Cuts anywhere on the head, even small ones, may bleed profusely, frightening the victim and those giving first aid. To control bleeding from a cut on the scalp, make a "ring pad" by wrapping a long bandage around all four fingers of your hand, creating a

Head injuries are the most common type of injury.

doughnut-shaped ring. Remove the ring from your hand, position it around the edges of the wound (not directly on it), and apply pressure. If the cut is large or will not stop bleeding, stitches may be needed.

The symptoms of head injuries that require medical care include loss of consciousness; confusion; memory loss; drowsiness; a dent, bruise, or cut on the scalp; severe headache; stiff neck; vomiting; blood or spinal fluid (a clear liquid) coming from the mouth, nose, or ear; changes in vision; pupils of unequal size; convulsions; or the inability to move any part of the body or weakness in an arm or leg. These symptoms may begin right after the injury or may come later, and may indicate a concussion, contusion (a cut or bruising of the brain), or skull fracture.

From peewee football to professional baseball, the players of sports wear protective gear.

The Unconscious Patient

Any person who has been "knocked out" by a blow to the head should be treated as if he or she has a back or neck injury. It is extremely important to keep the victim still until professional medical help arrives. Any movement of the head, neck, or back could result in paralysis or death, so do not move the victim unless he or she is in immediate danger—from fire, for example.

Do not remove any protective gear the victim is wearing, including a helmet or shoulder pads. If the victim needs CPR or rescue breathing and is wearing a helmet with a face mask, the face mask should be cut away or unscrewed, leaving the helmet on the victim's head. A person who loses consciousness or experiences any of the symptoms of serious injury (listed above) should receive medical attention as soon as possible.

Danger of Bleeding

Another consequence of head injury is **intracranial bleeding** (bleeding inside the skull or the brain). This can be extremely dangerous and is one of the reasons that *all head injuries should be evaluated immediately by medical personnel.*

Intracranial bleeding is of two types: **arterial** (bleeding from an artery, which causes rapid blood loss) and **subdural** (bleeding from a vein, which is much slower). A person with arterial bleeding may be unconscious briefly, wake for several minutes or even several hours and seem fairly normal, then lose consciousness again and perhaps die if treatment is not prompt. Subdural bleeding is slower and may cause gradual deterioration over several hours or days.

A serious aspect of any head injury is brain swelling, which increases pressure in the skull and can cause unconsciousness, weakness, or paralysis if the nerves affecting the head, neck, and body are involved. Unless dealt with immediately, deterioration can set in and breathing may stop, resulting in possible brain damage and death.

In every case of serious head or neck injury,
remember:

- Keep the person calm and quiet until medical help
  arrives.
- In the case of a less serious injury, get medical care
  as quickly as possible.
- Give no fluids or food—these could complicate diagnosis or surgery.
- Be prepared to deal with an emergency and know
  how to get medical help.
- Keep yourself calm and alert.

Chapter 3

Neck Injuries

Some neck injuries are not serious. Even nonathletes can get a stiff neck simply by sleeping in an awkward position. Practicing your serve or throwing a ball can cause fatigue or spasm to the muscles in your neck. When this happens, the best way to get relief is to stretch your neck in the opposite direction.

Strains and sprains of the ligaments of the neck are possible, but rest and use of a cervical collar to support the head and neck will help. Tightness or spasm of the muscle, which occurs when there is bleeding in the muscle and no way for the blood to escape, is a warning of injury.

One type of injury is the **stretching of the neck muscles**. This can happen when you block or hit someone or something with your head, injuring some of the muscles and nerves leading to the shoulders and arms. The pain resembles a series of electric shocks in the neck and arms, and you may experience a weakness in those areas. Permanent weakness can result if the injury is not treated.

Broken Neck

The first seven bones of the spine are called the cervical vertebrae. A break, or fracture, of these bones (usually referred to as a broken neck) is always serious because it could result in damage to the spinal cord and possibly lead to paralysis. Dislocation of the neck (slippage out of normal alignment) does not always involve fracture, but it too can cause permanent damage to the spinal cord.

Whenever a neck injury is suspected, the victim should not be moved unless his or her safety is in immediate danger. For example, from a fire or possible explosion. Extreme caution in the way the victim is handled and prompt treatment for his or her injuries are necessary to prevent further injury and provide the best chance for recovery. If the victim is conscious, be sure that he or she does not try to get up or roll over. Do not the lift the victim's head to place a cushion under it. Use rolled towels or clothing to support the head on both sides, being careful to keep the head, neck, and back perfectly still. If the victim is wearing a hat, helmet, or other protective gear, do not remove it. If the injured person must be moved, one person should hold the victim's head in place with one hand on each side. Do not allow the person's head to move from side to side or to nod up and down. Then, with one person holding the head, several more people should lift the victim onto a stretcher or rigid board, being very careful not to jostle the head, neck, or back.

Breaking your neck is more than just an expression. It's very easy to do if you are hit when your neck is in the wrong position. Many people who land on their head diving into shallow water or being thrown from a horse break their neck. You can break your neck playing football if you hit someone with your head, or someone hits your head, hard enough.

Those seven bones, or vertebrae, can literally explode, causing a dangerous injury; this small area of the backbone is not able to protect the spinal cord as well as it does in the rest of your back. The danger is that when these bones break the spinal cord will tear or separate, causing paralysis.

This is why the head tackle is illegal in college and high school football. Helmets may decrease the danger of head injuries, but remember that your neck is still the weakest point between your helmet and your shoulder pads!

Chapter 4

Back Injuries

A back injury may be as simple as a muscle strain or sprain that requires you to limit activity, or as serious as a direct blow or unusual force to your back, resulting in permanent injury and needing extended therapy.

Young athletes may have a tendency to think that their back is indestructible. And why not? It has taken a lot of abuse and you're still walking around! Let's face it, when you're competing or practicing, with the coach and others watching, you tend to forget how you felt when you woke up this morning. Your neck and legs may have been sore, your back may have ached, and you didn't want to move! You might have been tempted to tell the coach you just couldn't make it today.

The Vulnerable Back

It doesn't take much **strain** or overexertion to

When your coach and the fans are watching you play, it is tempting to try to do just a little more and strain your back.

injure your back, especially if you are already
tired. It's easy to think you can do just a little more
(sports psychologists call this "stinkin' thinkin'").
So you try one more set of tennis, one too many
pass blocking drills, or that particular gymnastic
routine. Or you arch your back to strengthen it for
wrestling. Or maybe you try to lift too much
weight, or too much weight too soon—before
you're warmed up. Then your muscles tighten up
and you have strained your back.

Now you are probably lying in pain and
wondering what happened. In all likelihood, you've
torn your muscle fibers and they're bleeding into
the muscle itself. This irritates and inflames the
muscle, which responds by tightening up. Back
muscles are real "monsters"—sometimes up to
two inches thick. And when they tighten up on
you, you'll know it.

When that happens, you're out of commission.
You can't move. An antiinflammatory medication
will help. So will an ice pack, if the pain was
immediate. The cold will help to keep the swelling
down and slow the bleeding.

If the pain came later, heat may help. Stretching
the muscles while sitting in a hot tub could be just
the thing. If you're bending to the left side, stretch
to the right and vice versa.

Ways to Ease Pain

But what if the pain is in your lower back? One

way to stretch, if you can manage it, is to lie down, grab your thighs, and curl up, bending your head and shoulders in. Another way is to slowly bring one leg at a time to your chest.

If the pain is really bad, just lie down and bend your knees; that will move your pelvis up and gently relieve the strain. If that's too painful, try lying on your back with your feet on a pillow.

If you can't bear to lie down, try slowly bending at the waist and coming as close to touching a toe as possible. That will probably feel great, but the trick is straightening up afterward. Try bending your knees first and then straightening up.

The important thing is to do these exercises slowly and consistently, and as soon as possible, to get relief from the spasm and the resulting pain. Do them every ten minutes for a while, then go to twenty, thirty, and so on. Eventually, just stretching before going to bed should be enough. And remember, these same stretching exercises also work well as warm-ups before exercising or competing. When used in this way, they can keep you from re-injuring yourself.

At other times, it may not be a back injury that causes your back pain. Perhaps you bruised your heel on a stone while running. Your natural tendency would be to compensate by walking on the ball of your foot. Your body would adjust to this by twisting itself and sending the back muscles into a spasm.

Self-care begins with the realization of what has

happened to you. You can't fix it until you know what's wrong. Start by stretching your back muscles. Curl-ups should also be done. They are important because they strengthen your stomach muscles, which serve as a stabilizer for your back.

To do this important exercise, lie on your back and rest your hands on your chest. Be sure to keep your knees up and your back flat on the floor. Tilt your pelvis pressing your back flat, then *slowly* curl your head and shoulders up off the floor. Hold, then slowly curl back down. Do about three sets of five if you can. They are tough to do, so don't get discouraged if you can't get up to five. One curl-up equals 15 sit-ups. The important thing is to keep trying. If you do, the benefits will come.

When you're hurting less, you can slowly move into your regular routine. If you continue stretching and strengthening your back and stomach muscles, you'll help prevent a recurrence.

Knowing Your Limits

It is also important to know your limits, because one of these days your back may send signals that say, "This is serious! It's time to consult your doctor." Pay attention to these warnings:

- Back pain that goes into your arm, leg, or groin
- Numbness, tingling, or strange sensations in your arms or legs

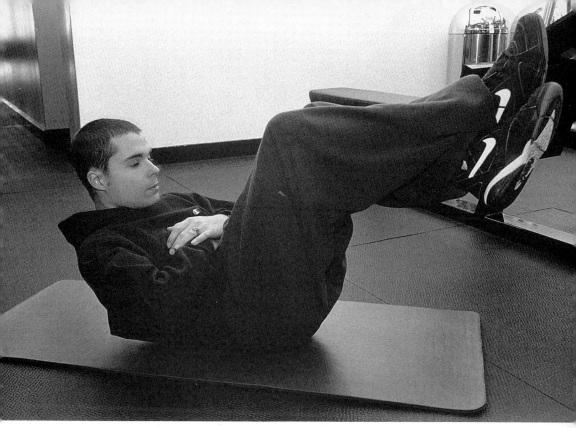

Sit-ups, curl-ups, or crunches strengthen your stomach, which then helps relieve stress and pressure on your back.

- Weakness in your arms or legs
- Coughing, sneezing, or other straining—like a bowel movement—that makes the pain worse

If you experience any of these symptoms, you could have an injury that involves nerve damage. If so, consult your doctor immediately! It makes no difference whether an injury is sudden or the result of overuse; these symptoms may indicate that your spinal column has been damaged, which is among the most dangerous injuries you can have.

Slipped Disk

Another type of back injury is one that involves

the **disks**. Your backbone runs from the bottom of your head to your tailbone. It contains over 30 separate vertebrae (bones) connected by ligaments, with disks between the vertebrae. Your spinal cord runs down the center of your backbone. It sends signals back and forth between your brain and your body. The disks are like spacers that absorb shock between the bones. The outside of the disks is tough, and the inside is gelatin-like.

When you have an injury that moves one of these little shock absorbers, the disk may move to one side or it may lose some of its fluid and become stiff. This is called a ruptured or slipped disk. The damaged disk may put pressure on the spinal cord, causing severe pain and loss of nerve function. It may even affect bladder or bowel control. It could cause permanent paralysis.

Treatment for a disk problem ranges from complete rest to medication to deal with inflammation and swelling. When all else fails, it may be necessary to remove a damaged disk surgically. This is called a laminectomy.

Stress Fracture

One back problem that results from overuse or misuse is a **stress fracture** (small, hairline break). This injury seems to result from overarching the back. Gymnasts may incur this injury during a dismount, and football linemen can get it coming out of position to block. It can also happen anytime the backbone is compressed as in pole vaulting, weight lifting, or jumping on a trampoline.

Once again, the simplest solution can be straightening your backbone and strengthening your stomach muscles. These fractures usually heal themselves with a long rest.

Another back injury is a **contusion** (result of a direct blow that causes blood vessels to bleed into the muscle). These injuries are common among football players. They usually happen when a player is hit with a knee, an elbow, or a helmet or is knocked on his back. They are treated in the same way as neck contusions (see above).

The main thing to remember about back injuries is to catch them early and pay attention to pain. Pain is the way your body tells you to stop and take care of yourself. It's not weakness—it's just good sense. Find out what's happening and take care of the problem!

Chapter 5

Arm, Shoulder, and Hand Injuries

P laying any of the throwing games—baseball, basketball, football, even bowling—requires us to move our arms, elbows, wrists, and shoulders in the same way over and over. No wonder so many injuries affect those parts of the body. Besides the sports mentioned, we play hockey, golf, racquetball, and tennis. We also lift weights, swim, ride bikes, row boats, and do gymnastics. Each repetitive movement can set us up for injury—and falls and blows can cause injury to these sensitive areas.

Your shoulders, arms, wrists, and elbows are the most flexible parts of your body. While this enables you make the movements required to dress, it also makes it easy to injure these body parts—and life after such an injury is frustrating. Simple things like combing your hair, brushing your teeth, or just getting dressed can be a problem.

Because of the flexibility of joints such as the shoulders and wrists, it is easier to injure these body parts.

Tennis Elbow

The single biggest factor in sports injuries is the way we use our muscles. Our muscles come in pairs, and we usually overuse one set while underusing the other. The kind of injury people get depends on which set they use in the sport they play.

An example is **tennis elbow**—the result of the backhand stroke used in playing tennis. When you use your wrist without using the rest of your arm, the strain on your wrist muscles is often too much; it may cause the other end of those muscles, attached to the inside of the elbow, to become inflamed, torn, or separated.

A similar injury is **Little League elbow**. In children and youths, the muscles on the inside of the elbow are not very strong. One hard throw can injure them.

These injuries take quite a while to heal. Usually, antiinflammatory medication, ice, and rest will help. Strengthening exercises help to prevent a repeat injury. Using equipment with larger grips and less weight will also help. It is equally important to learn to throw properly and only when necessary.

Forearm, wrist, and hand injuries can be serious and should be treated by your doctor. They may require x-rays, splints, and casts. Do not try to ignore the pain and swelling. Don't try to treat yourself. Injuries can include fractures (broken bones), carpal tunnel syndrome, nerve compression, contusions, and sprains. As usual, ice, antiinflammatory medication, and rest (for up to six weeks) are the best treatments.

Carpal Tunnel Syndrome

With an injury like **carpal tunnel syndrome** or **carpal tunnel fracture**, failure to seek medical attention could leave you permanently injured. Numbness or tingling of the first three fingers can be a sign that you have this type of injury. It is caused by overuse of your hand and wrist and is treated with medication, splints, exercise, and temporarily stopping the activity that caused the injury. If this doesn't work, surgery may be necessary.

If the numbness or tingling is in your fourth and fifth fingers, you may have injured your **"funny bone"** or overused your wrist. Called an **ulnar nerve compression**, it is treated with rest and by switching to better equipment.

Although a sprained finger or wrist may need to be x-rayed, taped, or put in a splint, a dislocated finger may take longer to heal to avoid permanent damage.

Contact Sport Injuries

Shoulder and upper arm injuries are a hazard in

all contact sports. For instance, football and hockey players can experience a shoulder separation because of stretched or torn ligaments connecting the shoulder to the collarbone. A shoulder separation (partial tear) can heal in a few days by putting the arm in a sling. A complete separation usually requires surgery.

Baseball players and fans have heard of the torn or inflamed **rotator cuff** that pitchers suffer. The rotator cuff is a set of three muscles that hold together the **humerus** (the main bone of the shoulder) and the **scapula** (shoulder blade).

Surprising to most athletes, the shoulder joint is like a golf ball resting against a small saucer. The only thing holding it there is a few muscles and tendons. That's why shoulders are so easy to twist and swing—and why they're so easy to injure. When your shoulder is out of commission, you're not only out of the tennis match, track meet, or basketball game, you're suddenly out of all your daily activities—even opening doors, buttoning shirts, lacing shoes, or lifting a glass to your mouth.

One of the most common shoulder injuries is a broken **clavicle** (collarbone). This can be caused by a direct blow or by reaching out to break a fall. The clavicle is not much thicker than a finger bone. It will hurt like crazy and swell, but after it's set, it should heal.

Contusions to the shoulder are seldom serious.

Sports such as boxing are more strenuous on certain parts of the body, like the shoulders.

They usually affect the **deltoid muscle** (the big muscle that caps your shoulder and protects the other muscles and tendons). If the deltoid muscle goes into spasm, you will overuse other muscles. This will cause you to learn new, unhealthy ways of playing your sport. These habits will be hard to break when your shoulder is well again. Another problem is that those substitute muscles won't be as strong, and further injury could be the result.

Strains

Strains are another common injury. When the **rhomboids** (muscles in the center of your back that hold the edge of your shoulder blade to your spine) go into spasm, you'll have little knots in the center of your back that are hard and painful. Help it by resting the muscle. You can also stretch it by "hugging" yourself, and strengthen it by leaning forward and folding your arms like wings and flapping them backwards.

If the **trapezius** (the big muscle that runs down your back to your waistline) goes into spasm, rest for a couple of hours. Then start stretching and strengthening it. Shoulder shrugs are a good way to do that.

A strain of the **triceps** (the muscle on the outside of your upper arm) is usually the result of overuse, usually from doing clean-and-jerk weight lifting, throwing, or hitting backhands. Resting from your sport, using ice, and correcting your form can lead to recovery.

Chapter 6

Leg and Knee Injuries

If your sport is track or basketball, you already know the importance of your legs and their muscles. Most leg injuries can be avoided by warming up, thereby avoiding running on your toes and preventing overuse.

Remember that overuse can be a result of favoring one muscle over another, but overuse injuries can also happen because of change. A change in stride, distance, speed, terrain, surface, or shoes can be enough to cause overuse injuries. So can returning too quickly to your sport after being sick. Because muscles deteriorate quickly, they must be reconditioned before full-fledged competition.

Importance of Prevention

Prevention is the key here. Since tightness in the calf is a common leg problem, try this stretching exercise several times a day: Put your palms on the wall and your heels flat on the floor about thirty inches from the wall; with your knees and arms straight, push your stomach to the wall.

Your lower leg has two bones, the **tibia** (the largest bone in the lower leg, which supports 80 to 90 percent of your body's weight), and the **fibula** (the smaller of the two bones in the lower leg). The leg muscles are divided by thick tissue into compartments. Those are called the anterior, superior, posterior, deep posterior, and lateral.

Acute compartmental syndrome is the name given to pain or injury of these muscles, and it's almost always serious. When the muscles swell, blood flow to these compartments is restricted. It may take major surgery to correct this. The best thing to do is stop running before it gets that bad. Severe pain with tingling and numbness are present when you move your ankle or toes. If you have enlarged leg muscles and gradual pain while running, you probably have **chronic compartmental syndrome**, which may respond to a lower level of activity or may require surgery to relieve the pressure.

Your doctor may diagnose **deep posterior compartmental syndrome** by measuring pressure in the compartment with a Wick Catheter. The pain may last for several hours after exercising and be accompanied by tingling and numbness. Surgery will be required. **Stress**

fractures are something else not to be ignored. They show up when you're pulling on your sock and notice pain.

Stress Fractures

If you can spot tenderness when you run your finger down your shin but nothing shows up on an x-ray, you may have stress fracture (the bone has bent almost to breaking and has a hairline crack in it).

This can also result from a change in your routine or activity. Your bones react to force or stress in an odd manner. As you increase the stress on a bone, new bone doesn't simply grow on top of the old. Instead, the bone starts removing old bone so that new bone can grow. This means that the bone is not as strong as it would be normally.

Before things get serious, find a level of activity as heavy but as pain-free as possible. In this way, you'll be conditioning the bone to heal so it will be ready when you resume your original level of activity. Go slow and don't push too far. It takes time for bone to disappear and rejuvenate. Three weeks into recovery, you should slow down for ten to fourteen days.

True fractures are something you can't treat yourself. But be sure that your doctor gives you good rehabilitation exercises (so you won't come out of the cast with stiff, useless legs).

Shin Splints

Shin splints occur when muscles pull away from the **shinbone**. You'll know you've got them if the area hurting is about twelve inches long on the front part of your lower leg. Treatment is a matter of trial and error, including taping the leg, using arch supports or heel inserts, applying ice, and taking antiinflammatory medication. Strengthening and stretching the lower leg muscles is one of the first things to do. Try attaching some rubber tubing to a board, putting your foot on the board, then pulling the tubing upward with your arms and hands. Your toes should curl slightly downward. Change the slack in the tubing as stretching increases, and do some calf stretching before and after.

Knee Injuries

The knee is involved in more than 25 percent of all sports injuries and 75 percent of those requiring surgery. An engineering miracle, the knee is flexible enough to bend 150 degrees front to back, about 4 degrees to the side, and to rotate 90 degrees. It withstands pressures up to 2,000 pounds and is self-lubricating.

The knees are the source of so many injuries because they are subjected to a lot of abuse. Although they are large joints, many things can go wrong with so much bone, the thickest **cartilage**

in the body, seven separate **ligaments**, one huge
tendon and several smaller ones, and many **bursa**
(sac-like cavities between joints).

Boys between the ages of 10 and 14 are especially
prone to two kinds of knee injuries. The first type of
injury is called **Osgood-Schlatter**. Although the
cause of it is not certain, overuse is usually a factor.
This results in a pulling on the kneecap tendon, which
causes the near end of the tibia (the front bone in the
lower leg) to fragment at the point where the tendon
attaches. When the knee is bent, pain develops just
below the patella (kneecap). This makes you want to
walk and run with a stiff leg. The condition clears up
on its own with rest, limited exercise, and protective
knee pads.

The second injury is called **osteochondritis
dessicans**, which is as hard to pronounce as it to
put up with. Symptoms include pain, swelling, a
lump over the knee, and knee-locking. When the
knee gets knocked around enough, a part of the
bone inside dies and the cartilage over the knee
separates and falls into the joint. Depending on
how early it is diagnosed, your doctor may
recommend immobilization (locking the knee
permanently) or surgery to remove the cartilage.

Overuse of Muscles

Although you may be tired of hearing about
overuse as a cause of injury, many athletes do

overuse their bodies and pay the price for doing
so. Tendinitis, bursitis, and synovitis are three
more examples of overuse. While they can be
caused by a blow to the knee, most doctors
believe they are usually caused by too much use
too soon—too much running, kicking, and
exercise.

With **tendinitis**, you'll find that rest, ice, and
antiinflammatory medication will help relieve the
pain and tenderness. You will aggravate it if you
continue to exercise—and you will hear a grinding
noise whenever you do. Sprinters and weight
lifters may get tendinitis in the quadriceps (the
large muscle on the front of the upper leg).
Athletes who jump too much can get it in the
patella (kneecap)—called "jumper's knee." Long-
distance runners get it in the hamstring (the large
muscle at the back of the upper leg).

Tenderness and a grating sensation along with
swelling may mean **bursitis**, an inflammation of
the bursa (a small sac filled with lubricating liquid
that reduces the friction between tendons and
bones). Bursitis can become chronic (permanent)
if the knee is abused long enough. The
result is heavy-duty pain and swelling. The best
treatment is drainage and an injection of cortisone.
Basketball players and athletes who fall on
artificial turf may get **prepatellar bursitis**
(swelling in the sac under the kneecap). This will
probably need to be drained by medical personnel.

On the other hand, wearing protective pads can usually prevent the injury.

Synovitis is swelling and inflammation of the membrane lining the knee joint. If this condition becomes serious, you will probably need to see an orthopedic surgeon. An **arthroscope** is a tiny telescope with a light and video camera that is inserted into the knee through a 1/4-inch cut. This is a very expensive operation and may not be necessary if your doctor thinks that rehabilitation and treatment could take care of your problem.

Another thing to consider is that after surgery you may never get back to your original level. You may lose 10 percent or more of your playing ability. Surgery is always a risk, no matter how miraculous it may seem. Remember, a Joe Montana may come back after surgery and seem to play as well as he ever did. But he started out better than the average player, he makes his living playing, and he's aware of the trade-offs—like future problems. High school athletes don't get the same kind of medical attention, and they don't get an around-the-clock personal trainer, either! Also, you may not be willing to spend up to half your time in rehabilitation for six to ten months after surgery.

Sprained ligaments can be caused by sudden turning of the knee or a violent twist of the body after a lower leg blow. The sprain may be mild, or involve a complete rupture of the **medial**

It is important to stretch the hamstrings and calves before exercising.

meniscus (a disk that cushions bone in a joint). Mild cases can be treated with ice and rest, but severe cases require a cast or surgery.

Whether caused by wear and tear, sudden twisting, or a blow to the knee, either of the two cartilages can be torn. The symptoms are pain or swelling, locking, or popping sounds in the knee. In this case, you will need to see an orthopedic surgeon for diagnosis and treatment.

Dislocated Kneecap

A dislocated kneecap is a very painful injury. It can be caused by a fall, weak ligaments around the kneecap, or a blow to the knee. If you dislocate a kneecap, you will not be able to straighten your leg. There will be a bulge on the side of your knee. Your doctor will put a cast or splint on it to allow it to heal, and with luck you won't need surgery. If you break a kneecap, you will notice swelling in the knee and a crunching feeling. An x-ray will be needed to confirm the fracture. If so, your orthopedic surgeon will take it from there.

He or she might recommend strengthening exercises to condition your leg. A weighted shoe, weighing about five pounds, would be as effective as a gym machine.

In the upper leg, the **femur** (thighbone that runs from the hip to the knee) is the longest and strongest bone in your body. The muscles (quadriceps in front and hamstring in back—also called the **adductor** and **abductor**) move your hips and knee joints.

The **quadriceps** is your body's most powerful muscle. It gives you power and speed. The three hamstring muscles straighten your hips and bend your knees. They are very important for runners.

Running

Runners remember: Beware overdeveloping your quadriceps and neglecting your hamstrings— you may find yourself with pulled muscles. The next time you run, they will put you in severe pain. When that happens, don't continue to run! If you do, you'll end up with bleeding muscles. For hamstrings, you should try a compression wrap, ice, massage, and gentle stretching for a few days. For quadriceps, you may need to do this for three weeks. Later, rest and heat could help both. It will take about six weeks to recover completely.

A **charley horse** is a muscle contusion or bruise that usually involves the quadriceps. A running back can get one from being tackled. If the bruising is bad, the muscles swell and the knees lose range of movement. Bruising causes muscle tightness and pain when the muscle cools down. You may have to treat it with ice and a compression wrap and rest for a day or two. You may also need to wear a hard thigh pad for protection. And when you get back on the field, don't push yourself.

Sometimes, after a really bad contusion, you may get **myositis ossificans** (bones forming in the muscle and connecting tissue). This can cause a great deal of pain and swelling, and often lasts for weeks at a time. You will need to rely on your doctor's advice and do only as much as you can bear. Exercise and massage won't help. At the worst, you may have three to six months of disability.

If you notice pain along the side of your knee that doesn't ease when you are running and a noticeable tightness all along your thigh, you may have a tight **iliotibial band** (the strongest and longest ligament in your body). Rest, ice, and antiinflammatory medication should help. A wrap won't help—and could make it worse. Stretching exercises can help prevent recurrence.

Overdoing running on hard surfaces can result in stress fracture of the **femur** (the thigh bone). Don't ignore this, because it can become a complete fracture. Immediate treatment is needed. It can be an emergency because of serious blood loss and shock, as well as major swelling and pain. A bone scan (instead of an x-ray) can confirm the injury. Rest for about six weeks usually helps.

Chapter 7

Hernias

A hernia (a bulge of soft tissue that forces its way through or between muscles) is not usually as serious as some people think. Weak or torn muscles allow the tissue to push out. The only symptom is usually swelling, which can form slowly over several weeks, or suddenly while lifting a heavy weight. You may feel a tenderness, or perhaps a "dragging" or heaviness.

Hernias are most common in the abdominal wall (muscles and fat that cover the stomach, intestines, liver, and kidneys). The most common type for athletes is an **inguinal hernia** (one that occurs in the groin). Some hernias can be pushed back into place with no problem. If not, your doctor will probably recommend surgery to take out the hernia sac and shorten or bring together the weak muscles. He or she will also tell you to take it easy for about a month and do no heavy lifting.

If a hernia involves the intestine, the contents of the intestine will not be able to pass through and you will have pain, nausea, and vomiting. This is called an **obstructed hernia**. If the hernia swells and cuts off the blood supply to the intestine, the strangulated hernia becomes red, extremely painful, and enlarged. It requires emergency surgery.

Other types of hernias include **femoral** (upper thigh), **epigastric** (centered just below the breasts), and **paraumbilical** (belly-button). The important thing to remember is that most hernias can get worse. The danger, especially with a groin hernia, is that intestinal strangulation will occur. Surgery and following your doctor's orders will get you back on your feet as soon as possible.

Chapter 8

Preventing Sports Injuries

Preventing sports injuries is one of the most important things any athlete will ever do. Any professional athlete will tell you the same thing, "You can't play if you aren't well!" By now, you know that thousands of athletes your age are injured every year. Before you become one of them, or become one of them again, read and apply the principles in this chapter. They work!

Injury prevention includes conditioning, training, performing—and a whole lot more! Being in shape is great. So is understanding your sport. Does that mean you're ready to go out there and show them your stuff? Not yet!

Condition Your Body for Your Sport

Far too many athletes who are in excellent shape are injured every year. Sometimes it's because they didn't take conditioning seriously. Conditioning means getting your body in shape *for your particular sport.* It takes very different approaches to condition your body for the games of football, basketball, and baseball. The reason? Each sport makes very different demands on your body.

Conditioning for football and gymnastics are as different as the rules for each sport. When you understand conditioning as a way of being ready, you have accepted the idea that you have to be physically able to answer the demands your sport makes on you. Some sports require explosive, short bursts of energy, whereas others require endurance. Football players can "run" several plays in an hour-long game with a lot of short rests, but few if any could run a marathon.

"Appropriate" conditioning means not only that you're able to compete successfully, but that the program is right for you at your stage of growth. An overintensive conditioning program can get you injured before you ever have a chance to compete.

Good conditioning workouts build stamina *and* endurance, strength *and* muscle tone. You should gain greater agility *and* flexibility, better coordination *and* balance. Where you start depends on what your physical and emotional limits are at your age.

Condition from Your Baseline

Remember, all great athletes condition. They start by finding out what they are able to do, *now*. This is called an "athlete's personal baseline" (APB). It is their own personal starting point. Professional athletes know better than to start training at someone else's baseline.

Imagine a professional athlete being stupid enough to start lifting at Walter Thomas's baseline? Walter may be the world's greatest power lifter. His record 2,050 pounds in three lifts—squat, bench, and dead lift—may never be broken. A fool who tried to start lifting at such a level—would end up with a crushed chest, a broken back, and all his leg muscles ripped loose. So all athletes must find their APB.

Then they *gradually* increase the level and intensity of their workouts. This is the principle of *progressive differentiation*. If you want to run ten miles and your APB is one mile, try running one and a half miles. When you've mastered that, run two miles. Your success depends on you—your ability, your maturity, and your commitment—and on realistic, reasonable goals that are right for you.

Plan Your Workout

You need to plan your workout. Divide each one into four parts: warm-up, skills practice, sport-related practice, and cool-down. The warm-up increases blood flow to your muscles and stretches your tissues for maximum flexibility. Fifteen minutes of vigorous exercise raises muscle temperature to about 103 degrees, which warms up all the major muscle groups in the legs, arms, back, hips, and torso.

Because most sports have specific skills, this is the main part of your workout. Don't concentrate on more than one or two skills in each workout. If your sport is one that does not require several skills, then speed, distance, or endurance will be what you work on.

Next, spend a few minutes actually playing your sport. It makes little difference whether you call this phase "scrimmage," "practice match," "volleying," or "batting practice." The point is, all athletes get turned on and tuned in by playing their sport. Without this component in your training program, you won't feel enthusiastic or focused. And that's dangerous. Athletes who are bored or distracted are candidates for injury.

Then it is time for the cool-down phase of training. This should last about 15 minutes. You should slow down but continue exercising—a brisk walk, gentle calisthenics, or cycling at a moderate pace are good cool-down exercises. Then hit the showers—warm is best, by the way.

The final step is just as important as the warm-up. After working out, your muscles should be tight. They need to be stretched and gently

exercised to get rid of the excess lactic acid
(which enters the blood with adrenaline during
exercise and signals an increase in heart rate).

One thing is common to all training: If you
do it right, you'll have less risk of injury. The
various injuries are specific to certain sports, and a
good training program will help prevent them. If
you're not sure your training is doing that, ask
your coach, trainer, or a sports medicine
specialist.

Train for Endurance and Power

There are two types of muscles: slow-twitch and
fast-twitch. If you have a lot of fast-twitch or fast-
firing muscles, you'll do better in sports that need
speed and intense power with short bursts of
energy. If you have more slow-twitch muscles,
sports that require endurance are best for you.
That doesn't mean that you should train only one
set of muscles. Endurance and speed are both
important in most sports, so your conditioning
should include aerobic exercise and anaerobic
training.

Understanding your body's energy-producing
ability means knowing something about its two
types of metabolism: increasing *aerobic metabolic
capacity* is the goal of endurance training. This
type of metabolism depends on oxygen to convert
energy. It is the type of training you should be

doing if your sport is long-distance running, bicycle racing, or basketball. You want to do things to train your body to have more endurance. Good exercises would be dance aerobics, running, swimming laps, speed-walking. If weights are used, you'll do weight lifting with lots of repetitions.

On the other hand, fuel for *anaerobic metabolism* is stored in the muscle fiber. This means that bursts of energy are produced that result in explosive activity. One goal of anaerobic exercise is training the muscles to resist the presence of lactic acid. A build-up of this chemical happens fast with high-intensity exercise, causing fatigue and muscle discomfort. Sports such as football, shot-putting, and power lifting are typical of this kind of metabolism. You need to include things like heavy weight lifting and sprinting in your training program.

Weight Train Sensibly

If weight training is a part of your training program, keep a few things in mind. Most weight lifting equipment is not made for people your age. Ten pounds can be too much of an increase for a new lifter. And increasing your lifts in large increments can set you up for injury by forcing you to develop bad lifting habits in trying to compensate. If you are a beginning lifter, you will need more supervision and instruction than friends who are more seasoned lifters.

Make sure the person teaching you to lift isn't fanatical. Some people think weight lifting is all there is to life! Don't let a fanatic push you too hard, making you attempt to lift weights you're not ready to lift. Trying to lift too much too soon can seriously damage your body, ripping apart bones, ligaments, cartilage, and muscles—sometimes permanently! And remember the basic rules for weight lifting:

1. Always warm up. (Weights are notorious for damaging cold muscles).
2. Stretch after lifting. (If you don't, you will become "muscle-bound," losing so much range of motion that you won't be able to move well.)
3. Never lift without a "spotter" (someone to help if you get into trouble during a lift—all pro lifters use one).
4. Only lift weight you can control (quivering means you're lifting too much).
5. Lift deliberately and come down the same way.
6. Work up to heavier weights gradually (remember the principle of progressive differentiation).
7. Use equipment that's the right size—or as close to the right size as possible—for you.
8. Don't hurry a lift (forced = loss of control).

9. Never lift two days in a row—alternate with aerobic workouts every other day.
10. Never arch your back, especially during the bench press.
11. BREATHE! Breathe out when you lift—"blow" the weight up—and breathe in as you bring the weight down to the starting position. (Holding your breath while straining to lift will dramatically increase your blood pressure and you could have a stroke or heart attack).
12. Don't ignore pain, especially in the joints. (If it is severe, or if it lasts more than a couple of days, stop lifting and see your team trainer or doctor immediately.)

Eat Like an Athlete

What you eat every day has a lot to do with how well you can compete and how well you can resist injuries. A longstanding myth had everyone thinking athletes really have to "chow down" before the "big game." Don't buy this. Eating too much before competing can be disastrous. A large part of your body's energy may be needed to digest the meal, leaving you feeling sluggish.

Most athletes relax before competing in order to conserve energy. What's important is to eat a balanced diet of high-energy and nutritious foods. The best sources for the calories you need are grains, dried fruits, breads, and pastas. These

Eating healthy foods helps keep your body in its best form.

foods, called "complex carbohydrates," are important because they contain minerals and glycogen. When you exercise, glycogen converts to glucose to make fuel for your muscles.

What happens when your muscles burn glucose? It forms a compound called pyruvate, which combines with oxygen to form carbon dioxide and water, which the lungs excrete. When the exercise is intense and strenuous, pyruvate changes to lactic acid because there's not enough oxygen. Your lungs can't get rid of that, the muscles won't contract, and you slow down. Even well-trained athletes can reach the point where their body can't get enough oxygen to the muscles, but they know when to slow down.

And don't forget to drink enough water. Dehydration causes lower muscle strength and cuts your level of glycogen.

There are no "magic" diets or vitamins that will improve your performance or guarantee you a successful career equal to that of your favorite sports star. In fact, certain vitamins or minerals can be dangerous if you take too much of them (vitamins A and D and iron are all poisonous in large amounts, and too much niacin can damage your heart). And never eat sugar-laden food during competition; it won't give you extra energy or strength, but it will force the blood into your stomach and intestines and may cause you to lose the competitive edge.

Protective Equipment

There is one basic rule about protective equipment: *Use what is appropriate for your sport.* Watch sport professionals in actual competition. You'll see batters wearing helmets, football players wearing everything from shoulder pads to face guards, basketball players wearing knee pads and protective goggles.

Why do you think the best players—many of them earning at least a million dollars a year— wear protective equipment? They got where they are by using their heads, and they want to live long enough to enjoy spending those millions!

Glossary

abdominal wall Muscles and fat that cover the stomach, intestines, liver, and kidneys.

abductor The muscle on the back of the thigh, running from the buttocks to the knee; also called the *hamstring*.

adductor The body's largest muscle, on the front and outside of the upper leg; also called *quadriceps*.

adrenaline Chemical that causes the body to become excited, increasing heart rate, blood pressure, energy level, and awareness.

arterial bleeding Bleeding from an artery, usually a large flow of blood.

arthroscope Tiny telescope with a light and video camera attached, used by orthopedic surgeons.

athlete's personal baseline Each athlete's point at which to begin training.

atrophy Process by which a body part dries up and becomes useless.

bursa Sac-like cavities between joints.

bursitis Inflammation of the bursa due to overuse.

carpal tunnel syndrome Pain in wrist and numbing of the first three fingers due to overuse.

cartilage Tough, elastic tissue that forms a part of the skeleton.

cervical vertebrae First seven bones of the spine, located in the neck.

chronic compartmental syndrome Dangerous condition that results in restricted blood flow in the lower leg muscles.

clavicle The collarbone.

concussion Violent jolt to the brain.

complex carbohydrates Energy foods such as bread, pasta, and dried fruits.

contusion Result of a direct blow that causes: (1) bruising of the brain, or (2) rupture of blood vessels and bleeding into a muscle.

disks Spacers that hold the vertebrae apart.

fast-twitch muscles Muscles that enable the athlete to have short, powerful bursts of energy.

femoral hernia Hernia of the upper thigh.

glucose Body sugar that combines with oxygen to form an essential part of the energy chain.

hernia Bulge of soft tissue that forces its way through or between muscles.

intracranial bleeding Bleeding inside the skull or brain.

lactic acid Chemical that builds up in muscles during and after exercise, making the muscles sore.

laminectomy Surgical removal of a disk from the backbone.

medial meniscus Disk that cushions bones in joints.

obstructed hernia Hernia that swells to the point that the contents of the intestines are blocked. Can lead to *strangulated hernia.*

Osgood-Schlatter disease Pulling of the kneecap tendon, which causes the tibia to fragment where the tendon attaches.

prepatellar bursitis Bursitis of the sac under the kneecap.

progressive differentiation The way in which athletes achieve training and recovery goals in small increments.

rotator cuff Set of three muscles that hold the humerus and scapula together.

shin splints Pain resulting from muscle pulling away from the lower front leg bone.

slow-twitch muscles Muscles that enable an athlete to have greater levels of endurance.

stress fracture Fine, hairline break of a bone.

subdural bleeding Bleeding from a vein; usually a very slow blood flow.

synovitis Inflammation and swelling of the membrane lining the knee joint.

tendinitis Overuse of the tendons causing inflammation and swelling.

trapezius Large muscle that runs down the back to the waist.

triceps Muscles that run down the outside of the upper arm.

vertebrae The approximately thirty bones that make up the backbone.

Where to Go for Help

Avoiding Injury
The best people to talk to about avoiding sports injuries are your physical education teacher, coach, trainer, or doctor. They are all trained in teaching people how to avoid injury. Your parents may also be able to help you develop and stick to an exercise program that will strengthen the muscles you need for your sport.

Dealing with Drinking and Drug Use
If you or a friend are using alcohol, steroids, or other drugs, there are many ways for you to receive free, confidential information and assistance. Groups such as Alcoholics Anonymous (AA) and Narcotics Anonymous (NA) exist to help people with concerns about alcohol and drug use. There is also special assistance available for children whose parents are substance abusers, through groups such as Al-Anon and Nar-Anon. You may call 1-800-ALCOHOL (1-800-252-6465) for information on programs and hotlines near you, or look in your area phone book for local groups.

Alcohol Hotline
(800) ALCOHOL (252-6465)

American Council for Drug Education
204 Monroe Street
Rockville, MD 20850

Narcotics Anonymous
(818) 780-3951

For Further Reading

Bar-Or, Oded, editor. *The Child and Adolescent Athlete*. Cambridge, MA: Blackwell Science, 1995.

Betz, Randal R., editor. *Child with a Spinal Cord Injury*. Rosemont, IL: American Academy of Orthopedic Surgeons, 1996.

Hawkins, Jerald D. *Sports Medicine: A Practical Guide for Youth Sports, Coaches and Parents*. Canton, OH: Professional Reports Corp, 1992.

Lukas, Scott E. *Steroids*. Springfield, NJ: Enslow Publishers, 1994.

Micheli, Lyle J., and Mark D. Jenkins, *Sportswise: An Essential Guide for Young Athletes, Parents and Coaches*. Boston: Houghton Mifflin, 1990.

Reider, Bruce, editor. *Sports Medicine: The School-Age Athlete*. Philadelphia: W. B. Saunders Co., 1996.

Sullivan, J. Andy. *Pediatric Athlete*. Rosemont, IL: American Academy of Orthopedic Surgeons, 1990.

Index

About the Author

Dr. Lawrence Clayton earned his doctorate from Texas Woman's University. He is an ordained minister and has served as such since 1972. Dr. Clayton is a clinical marriage and family therapist and certified drug and alcohol counselor. He is also president of the Oklahoma Professional Drug and Alcohol Counselors Certification Board. Dr. Clayton lives with his wife, Cathy, and their three children in Piedmont, Oklahoma.

Photo Credits

Cover by Lauren Piperno; pp. 2, 13 by Kim Sonsky; pp. 6, 11, 25, 29, 33, 42 by Michael Brandt; pp. 21, 56 by Marcus Shaffer; p. 14 © AP/Wide World Photo.